A I

50 THINGS EVERY GUY SHOULD KNOW HOW TO DO

DANIEL KLINE is a former editor of Uproar.com, Backslap.com, and Rouze.com, and has contributed to *Stuff, Playboy,* and other men's periodicals. He writes a syndicated newspaper column that appears in papers across the country.

JASON TOMASZEWSKI, a freelance writer, is a former football commentator and sports analyst.

50

THINGS EVERY GUY SHOULD KNOW HOW TO DO

Celebrity and Expert Advice on Living Large

Edited by
Daniel Kline & Jason Tomaszewski

A PLUME BOOK

PLUME
Published by Penguin Group
Penguin Group (USA) Inc., 375 Hudson Street, New York, New York 10014, U.S.A.
Penguin Group (Canada), 90 Eglinton Avenue East, Suite 700, Toronto, Ontario,
Canada M4P 2Y3 (a division of Pearson Penguin Canada Inc.)
Penguin Books Ltd., 80 Strand, London WC2R 0RL, England
Penguin Ireland, 25 St. Stephen's Green, Dublin 2, Ireland
(a division of Penguin Books Ltd.)
Penguin Group (Australia), 250 Camberwell Road, Camberwell,
Victoria 3124, Australia (a division of Pearson Australia Group Pty. Ltd.)
Penguin Books India Pvt. Ltd., 11 Community Centre, Panchsheel Park,
New Delhi – 110 017, India
Penguin Books (NZ), cnr Airborne and Rosedale Roads, Albany, Auckland 1310,
New Zealand (a division of Pearson New Zealand Ltd.)
Penguin Books (South Africa) (Pty.) Ltd., 24 Sturdee Avenue, Rosebank,
Johannesburg 2196, South Africa

Penguin Books Ltd., Registered Offices: 80 Strand, London WC2R 0RL, England

First published by Plume, a member of Penguin Group (USA) Inc.

First Printing, May 2006
10   9   8   7   6   5   4   3   2   1

Ⓟ REGISTERED TRADEMARK—MARCA REGISTRADA

LIBRARY OF CONGRESS CATALOGING-IN-PUBLICATION DATA

50 things every guy should know how to do : celebrity and expert advice on living
large / edited by Daniel Kline & Jason Tomaszewski.
     p. cm.
  ISBN 0-452-28665-4 (trade pbk.)
  1. Men—Life skills guides. I. Title: Fifty things every guy should know how to
do. II. Kline, Daniel E., 1944– III. Tomaszewski, Jason.
  HQ1090.A15 2006
  646.70081—dc22

                                                                2005034867

Printed in the United States of America
Set in Galliard

To our parents,
because there are still a few things
you can't learn from celebrities.

Contents

Contents

Contents

Introduction

Finding out who moved your cheese won't make you rich, busting sugar won't make you thin, and no set of rules will possibly trick you into marrying an ugly woman. "They" aren't organized enough to keep the natural cures away from you and if you need an owner's manual for yourself, you have problems that no book can possibly solve.

Just reading a book won't help you lose weight, make money, or become better looking any more than just buying a weight bench will make you stronger. Like late-night infomercials, most advice books promise things they can't possibly deliver and fail in a spectacular fashion.

No one has written about an easy way to make money, lose weight, or achieve endless happiness, for the simple reason that these things aren't easy. The secret way to achieve all of these things is exactly the same, no matter what you're wishing for: Work hard and get a little bit lucky.

Our appetite for easy answers in book form has become so great that people have become famous just by writing them. The best way to achieve fame seems to be either creating a fad diet that involves eating only one food or designing a philosophy that makes no sense to anyone except Madonna.

With *50 Things Every Guy Should Know How to Do*, we wanted to create an advice book in which people who actually know how to do stuff share information that you can really use. You wouldn't want Carrot Top to teach you how to perform open-heart surgery, but the man knows how to make people laugh. Similarly, you may not want to go to a ball game with Richard Simmons, but he's helped more people lose weight than a river of cabbage soup and the South Beach Diet put together.

We believe that every guy deserves to spend a day eating fine food, sipping expensive liquor, smoking a fancy cigar, and enjoying the company of a beautiful woman. We also feel he should never have to know how to catch his spouse cheating on him, file for bankruptcy, or protect his assets in a divorce. Unfortunately, since the latter happen to as many guys as do the former, this book covers all those topics.

50 Things Every Guy Should Know How to Do won't change your life, but it will help you enjoy the good moments more and get through the tough ones a little easier.

—Daniel Kline, Jason Tomaszewski

50
THINGS EVERY GUY
SHOULD KNOW
HOW TO DO

1

HOW TO GET DRESSED FOR A DATE

Carson Kressley, member of *Queer Eye
for the Straight Guy*'s "Fab Five"
As told to Annie Wilner

About the Expert: *Carson Kressley serves as the fashion expert on the popular television makeover show* Queer Eye for the Straight Guy. *In his professional life, Carson is an independent stylist who spent many years working with Polo Ralph Lauren in New York City, specializing in the design aspect of the men's sportswear division. He also supervised fashion styling for the company's national retail advertising campaigns. He is the author of* Off the Cuff: The Essential Style Guide for Men—and the Women Who Love Them.

A great general guideline for getting ready for a date is that it's really all about *appropriateness*. Figure out the situation you are going to be in, such as where you're going on the first date. You're not going to wear the same thing to a picnic on the beach as you would for a night at the theater.

So when you call a day or two before, let your date or girlfriend—if it's a woman—know what the plan will be for the evening. For guys, when you're taking that extra time and putting some thought into the relationship, your date will really appreciate your efforts.

Going on a date is kind of like going on an interview (well, not exactly)—you want to make the best possible first impression. A good rule of thumb is to overdress just a little bit and always wear a sports jacket.

A sports jacket or a blazer will really dress up any outfit, and once you get inside, like at a restaurant, you can take the blazer off. A fabulous all-purpose outfit is a casual pair of slacks (not jeans), a relaxed sports coat, a solid watch, and a great pair of loafers. Just no pleats, please, for your slacks, because they make almost everyone look dumpy and fat.

The details, baby

It's really all about details, details, details. A sharp watch—it doesn't have to be expensive, just something steel, or even a Swatch—a nice belt, and a great pair of shoes will make any outfit shine.

In the '90s, we got into a baggy trend, so most guys are not educated as to where an armhole should actually fall. Details of fit are actually very important. The shoulder of the sleeve should end at your shoulder or fall just a little bit over your shoulder. Your shirt or sweater should look like it's *made* for your body.

A fitted dress shirt is always an excellent choice. Buy from a department store where you can develop a relationship with a salesperson who will lead you in the right direction. If you have a long-term relationship with a salesperson, he or she will have an investment in finding fabulous outfits for you. And then you will have a fairy god-stylist—like me—all to yourself!

Below the belt

Details also matter in the areas that your date may or may not see. Boxers are hot! And by "boxers" I mean the guys with gloves. But I'm really going to go with boxer-briefs because they're comfortable, plus you get all the great bun-hugging qualities. If the date goes really well, it could be a bit weird or totally kill the moment if you're wearing tighty-whities. No offense, boys.

Like I say in my book *Off the Cuff*, a lot of men think that to look slim, you have to wear all black. But by doing so you can end up looking dreary and pale. I say, stick with monochromatic solids for the top and the pants. A nice alternative to black is a chocolate brown, which is flattering on everyone, so pair a chocolate brown sweater with brown pants, or a navy turtleneck with navy pants. Just keep the top and the bottom the same color.

Also, it's great to be in shape, but if you spend a lot of time at the gym, and you're super pumped-up, remember: You shouldn't have larger breasts than your date's.

What not to wear

I don't like to have too many no's in my vocabulary, but banana hammocks are always a fashion don't. Also, say nay to really tight European thong swimsuits. And also never wear sandals with socks. You have to ask yourself, "What would Jesus do?" He would not wear the two together. And say *no* to gauchos and clogs. These are bad!

In terms of texture, the first rule is, never wear anything sheer. My motto is if it feels good, wear it. You can never have too much cashmere.

Any crazy jacquard is probably too much. All traditional menswear should be fine—but jazz it up with color. Work with accessories and color.

Feel good, look good

How you look on the outside tells the world how you feel on the inside. You carry your clothing with you everywhere, and it tells people what you're about and who you are. It's your uniform.

When you wear a great outfit, you feel confident, and confidence breeds success. And there's nothing women find sexier than confidence.

2

HOW TO MAKE SOMEONE LAUGH

Carrot Top, comedian, product spokesperson
As told to Sandra Carr

About the Expert: *Carrot Top is one of the most popular and successful comedians in America. Each year he stars for fifteen weeks in Las Vegas at the MGM Grand, headlines another hundred plus concerts across the country, and makes dozens of television appearances. Thanks to becoming a celebrity TV pitchman for 1-800-CALL-ATT, he's a household name. (He got the job when he told them, "I love telephones.")*

It's hard to pinpoint exactly what will make a woman laugh. A guy has to have a little bit of charm, and you really can't teach charm.

If you're trying to be funny, one thing is for sure: Don't steal my act. Prop comedy just doesn't translate to funny in social situations, and it's even hard for other comedians to pull off. I've challenged comics to write me a prop and they couldn't.

Comedians have done plays on words, but writing a visual joke is something else. A rubber chicken isn't enough. I have to write my own material and make my own props, because no one sells what I need—like the paper-cup-and-string telephone with a third cup for call waiting. I'm happy not only that I have my own style but that I've been an original from the very start.

Be real

I think people in general like to laugh at things they can relate to. It's about shared experiences or thoughts, and it can be anything.

Here's a current example: the kid that just had sex with his teacher [the Debra Lafave case]—which is disgusting. Men and women have decidedly different opinions about the humor of that situation. Women think it's disgusting and guys are like, "Cool, how did that happen?"

I talked about that during a radio interview promoting one of my shows. I said, "I couldn't find a date, so I had to book a show. How sad, a fourteen-year-old kid in school nailed his teacher. Not only am I not getting any action; I definitely wasn't getting any when I was fourteen. So, that sucks."

The guys were laughing, but the girl wasn't.

"That's disgusting, though," the girl said. The guys were still laughing. "But that's nasty," she said.

And I said, "I know, it's nasty. I am just saying it is the truth." Sometimes the truth is really funny.

The Carrot Top experience

If you really want to get a woman to laugh, just tell her how rotten men are. Women love to hear how stupid we are.

I tell a joke every night in my show specifically about women and the guys laugh. Then the guys say, "Dude, stop! I'm not supposed to laugh at this." And then I reverse it and say something about men and then the whole crowd goes nuts.

I think the truth is, if you can share the experience of something that has happened to you, people will laugh. All the world is a prop.

3

HOW TO GET A WOMAN TO DATE YOU

Britney Rears, adult film star

About the Expert: *A fast-rising adult film star, Britney Rears had a breakout hit with her debut film,* Britney Rears: Wild Backstage Sex Party. *She travels the country and has made appearances on a variety of television and radio programs.*

Getting a girl interested in you, well, that's sort of easy, really. A guy who wants to attract me has to seem in charge and not be a pushover. All of us want a man who is in control—not an asshole, but a guy who is cool and confident. It's hard to get turned on by a guy who is not taking charge, but very easy to get hot for a guy who runs the show.

Look sharp

I love my man to look good, so clothes are important to me, but I'm much happier when the guy is naked.

I like a lot of looks, including a nice-fitting business suit. That turns me on. Just about everybody looks hot in a suit. Jeans and a white T-shirt work, too, especially on a lazy weekend lying around together.

Grooming is important, and not just in the obvious places. It's really important for a guy who wants to get with me to be trimmed neatly down there.

Tweezed eyebrows is too much. Have you been to L.A.? That's the least that the guys do here. They have perfect bodies and tans, wear makeup, and sometimes smell better than most girls that I know. That might be a bit *too* groomed.

Be funny

It's extremely important that a guy be funny. Who wants to hang around with a miserable person? If a guy is cool and can make me laugh, I'll probably want to go that extra mile for him to please him. Just don't make me laugh when we're in bed because that will kind of ruin it for me.

I go over the top all the time; I'm still young and can get away with it, and I like my man to be the same. I just don't want to bang a comedian.

Does money matter?

It doesn't take cash to impress me. I see guys with cash all the time and they bore me, so if you're on a budget, just do the little things, like make sure your clothes and hair are washed and you smell clean. That's a total turn-on regardless of what a guy wears. A rich guy in a suit with dirty hair or body odor will never get near me.

When to give up

It can be hard to tell the difference between hard to get and "leave me alone." But I'll let you in on a little secret: I really don't think that any girl is out of reach for most guys. Most girls want sex just as much as men do, but we don't always let on.

If you fade away after your first approach, then you aren't worth shit. Come back and hit me baby one more time. Be assertive and confident (but not a pest).

Just walk up to the girl and try to strike up a conversation, but don't use any stupid lines. A good approach, especially in a big city, is, "Hey, I'm new to the city and I think you're really cute and I'm just looking for somebody cool to go out to dinner and to the movies." Believe me when I tell you that most chicks will jump at a guy who can deliver this kind of line.

Don't forget to smile, be friendly, and remember to shave your balls.

Bad boys, bad boys

Girls love the thrill off trying to calm a wild boy. But it doesn't usually take us long to realize we're better off starting with a good guy in the first place instead of wasting our time trying to change someone.

Girls want a guy who is exciting in bed and not a boring bag of bones. Be a man and act like one, and don't take any shit. Otherwise you'll end up on the outside looking in at her banging somebody else.

It's okay to be nice, just don't let her push you around. Don't pretend to be some badass motherfucker, but don't be a wimp, either.

Don't try too hard

You might want to learn a little something about her before you introduce yourself, but not too much. Usually it's better to just chat with the girl and figure her out for yourself.

Make her want you. Blow her off every once in a while. Showing a girl that you care way more than she does is too sweet. Slow down and make her want you. Pull back a bit and let her approach you. Don't cave in so fast by being sweet, because that syrup will drown you.

Guys should realize that all girls really want the same thing. We want a guy who cares about us. Girls want to be loved, too.

Women want to be loved back. They want a bit of a hunt without a huge chase and, in the end, they just want security and reliability.

And remember that size doesn't matter at all—unless it's totally small. We all like a bit of freak in our gentlemen. Please her well and often and she's yours forever. Trust me on that one.

4

HOW TO COOK FOR YOUR WOMAN

Michael Symon, celebrity chef,
Food Network host
As told to Douglas Trattner

About the Expert: *Michael Symon is the chef/owner of Lola Bistro in Cleveland, Ohio. A Culinary Institute of America graduate, he has won numerous awards and his eatery was named one of* Gourmet *magazine's top fifty restaurants in America. Symon appears on the Food Network's* Melting Pot *show and was one of the chefs featured in* The Soul of a Chef *by Michael Ruhlman (Penguin, 2001).*

Men who know how to cook are automatically appealing to most women. If you can prepare a meal for a date early on, it immediately sets you apart from others.

Food is such a natural, sensual thing—for men and women alike—with its different textures and flavors. Depending on what you're eating, it can be a very hands-on experience, which is good. It's oral.

Cooking isn't as difficult as it appears. If you shop well, chances are your meal will be a success. Don't panic; buy good products.

Be creative, but familiar

My cooking style is Midwestern-driven, based on local, seasonal, sustainable ingredients. I try to be very approachable—familiar, but with a twist. I'll do something like foie gras bratwurst—diners who may not be familiar with foie gras but who are familiar with bratwurst may want to give this dish a try.

This familiarity will put a woman at ease and will work in your favor. Remember, it all starts with the right ingredients.

Women love lobster and oysters. They love strawberries and champagne, as well as caviar and champagne. When you put those combinations in your mouth they complement each other and really stimulate your palate.

Women like vegetables, beautiful fresh greens with a light vinaigrette, chicken, and pasta. (Eighty percent of the pasta we sell at my restaurant is ordered by women.) Mac and cheese with roasted chicken, and goat cheese and fresh rosemary are also winning meals. And always serve a rich, fudgey, chocolate concoction or crème brulee for dessert.

Stay away from big hunks of beef and heavy, rich, cream sauces. You don't want the person you are cooking for to be so full from dinner that they want to take a nap afterward. You'll also want to avoid organ meats: sweetbreads, foie gras, kidneys, liver, pork belly, and sausage.

If you do serve meat, I think it's a good idea to always slice it before serving. It makes a nicer presentation and it's easier to eat. Always take meat off the bone and remove the head from the fish.

Romance is in the effort

Probably the most romantic dinner I ever cooked for my wife was on the only year we ever closed the restaurant for New Year's Eve. I got lobsters, clams, crab legs, fresh artichokes, and fingerling potatoes. I made a very refined version of a clambake. I served it with a citrus butter. We sat on the floor in front of a fire and ate dinner and drank champagne. It was so simple. We ate everything with our hands, and it was wonderful.

An aside for the hopeless

If you're completely incompetent in the kitchen, go to one of your favorite local restaurants and buy everything from them. You just warm it up, serve it, and look like the star. You can be as honest or dishonest as you wish to be, but I recommend lying. Say you did it all yourself.

Familiarity

Cooking for a spouse is easier than cooking for a date, because you know the person better so there is not as much risk involved. You know their likes and dislikes. So you don't have to play everything so close to the cuff. But on the other hand, these dinners tend to be less romantic. Conversations tend to be more about work and family matters—it's harder to escape all that, but the conversation is a lot more honest.

With a date, you'll know if things have gone well if she's still there the next morning. In that case, I'm a big fan of poached eggs; I would do an eggs Benedict on a toasted muffin or biscuit with some nice prosciutto. Some fresh-squeezed orange juice. Some French roast coffee. Fresh fruits like pineapples and melons are also perfect for breakfast in bed.

Buying the Right Ingredients

On fish: A lot of people are afraid to cook fish. They don't know what to look for when buying fish. For some reason, there is less fear that we will buy a bad steak than a bad piece of fish.

Build a relationship with the people who sell you your fish. Learn how to check for good product: Make sure the fish is firm and that it doesn't smell like ammonia or lemon water. Ask the fishmonger what he likes. It is perfectly acceptable to ask him if you can smell the fish. Press on the flesh gently and make sure it's firm and elastic. Your fingerprint shouldn't remain in the flesh.

Always try to buy wild fish over farmed fish. Cook fish at 300 degrees until the internal temperature is 140 degrees. Let it rest a minute and serve. Fish is quicker to cook than meat.

On local product: It's wise to cook food that is prevalent where you live. As far as seasonal availability, most grocery stores now let you know where the product is from. Look for products that are grown as close to your home as possible. Organic tends to be more seasonally grown and is usually a better product.

Stay away from the huge brands of chicken. Instead, look for the Amish-raised or smaller-run operations. They tend be higher quality. Food is like anything else; you get what you pay for. If there are two different brands of chicken breasts side by side and one's $2 a pound more expensive than the other, chances are it's a better product.

Cheese plate: I look for artisanal cheeses. Strive for variety; serve a cow's-milk cheese, a goat's-milk cheese, and a sheep's-milk cheese. Vary the levels of pungency from mild to slightly pungent—I wouldn't go too pungent for a dinner date. Also, mix soft cheeses with semi-soft and firmer ones.

Serve with crostini, crackers, a nice fruit marmalade, and some spicy pecans, along with a nice port. Or, if you are serving French cheeses, pair them with wine from the same region. It seems as if the cheese is deliberately made to go with the wine. I stay away from whites.

It Starts With the Right Equipment

When you're buying equipment for the home kitchen, buy it as you need it, because it's better to buy one really nice piece of equipment at a time than to get a low price for a bunch of junk. Take your time and build your collection. It doesn't matter if everything matches; get good quality, as you need it.

Make sure you at least have one sharp, high-quality chef's knife. You can do 90 percent of all home cooking with your chef's knife. So instead of buying the whole block set of knives, take the money you would spend on the block and buy a good chef's knife.

Also, if you aren't good with a sharpening steel, it's a good idea to get an electric Chef's Choice sharpener. Run your knife through once a week and it will help keep a sharp blade.

I love the micro-plane zesters for grating hard cheeses and zesting citrus. It's probably my favorite kitchen gadget. You will also want to buy good-quality pans, such as Calphalon, All-Clad. Get hard anodized aluminum, stainless steel, or copper. Again, you don't need every single pan, but get a really nice sauté pan because that's what you're going to be using for 80 percent of your cooking.

5

HOW TO HAVE A THREESOME

Suzy Baer, author, *Step by Step Threesome*

> **About the Expert:** *Suzy Baer is the author of* Step by Step
> Threesome *and the owner of Stepbystepthreesome.com. She is
> an international expert on threesomes and other sex topics.*

Let's face it, in the vast majority of cases, it's the guys that
come up with this idea. If the female is the one with the
initiative or if both of you are interested in pursuing the threesome fantasy, you're one step ahead.

However, if you'd like to experience a threesome and you've
never discussed it with your partner, you might need some
guidelines to help you persuade her to participate in your
fantasy.

The first thing that you've got to take into consideration is
that women place a high value on the pair-bond. Women are
very apprehensive of anyone or anything threatening the health
and longevity of a relationship. For most women, a threesome
carries risks they're not eager to accept. The first giant obstacle
you'll face will be overcoming her insecurity.

Clearing obstacles

Besides the social conditioning she was raised with, there are
some obstacles that need to be cleared before she can be enthu-
siastic about inviting someone else into an intimate session. Any
woman who truly cares about you worries about the relationship, with all the classic fears and uncertainty about your love.
You have to understand that she often asks herself, "Does he love

me fully?" "Does he love only me?" "Does he really like me the way I am?" "Am I woman enough to keep him satisfied?" "Will he leave me for a younger/firmer/prettier woman?"

Filled with uncertainty and jealousy, she will defend her turf against all possible threats. The only responsible person to ease the above-mentioned issues is the male in the relationship. Happy, secure, confident women aren't very jealous.

Avoid making her insecure

If your partner is jealous, it might stem from your own behavior. If you recognize yourself in some of this behavior, your partner has every right to feel insecure about your relationship. The following things could trigger her insecurity:

You frequently express your dissatisfaction about her.
You constantly criticize her and never compliment her.
You flirt with every cute woman you see.
You stay out all night from time to time.
You habitually express your discontent with your life and your relationship.
You only touch her while having sex, and you don't express your love often.
You threaten to leave her.

Any of these types of behavior will rapidly turn into insecurity, resentment, and jealousy. The insecure woman's worst nightmare is the competition of another female for her relationship, and in this case the last thing she'll do is invite another woman into your bed.

Remember, your partner has to feel very secure of your relationship before she'll grant you a threesome. So make sure you never threaten your relationship. It doesn't matter how angry or upset you become. She needs to know that you guys are an item and nothing will ever break your bond.

Female security is the number-one point of consideration. If you want her to be sexually confident, you must work very hard to make her secure in your love. If you're serious about taking your sex life to a level where a threesome can occur, you'll need to make your partner so happy, so positive, so confident, and so secure in your love that she's unafraid to share you with another woman.

What to do (and not do)

Compliment her and show her how much you love her on a regular basis. Write her loving cards, buy her flowers, cuddle up with her on the sofa, whisper in her ear how beautiful she is; there are a lot of small things you can do that have major positive impacts. Feeling loved, accepted, and secure is a powerful female aphrodisiac. She'll be much more loving if she feels you're happy with her.

Avoid silly remarks about her looks at all costs, especially if they're things she cannot change. Avoid telling her that she's fat. Instead of making negative remarks, try to compliment her as often as possible.

Don't flirt with her friends unless you've got her approval; if she believes your threesome is just a devious plot to bonk her best friend, you've got no chance of ever pulling it off.

Before you tell her about your desire to have a threesome, you must be sure she's certain that a threesome isn't threatening her relationship with you.

Persuasion

It may very well be that your lover fantasizes about a threesome, too, but has been afraid or embarrassed to admit it. Unlike men, women seldom speak to the point and often beat around the bush before telling you what they actually want. If you want her to talk about her fantasies, you can encourage her by:

1. Listening to her. Magic words for women are "Interesting, please tell me more." Then all you need to do is shut up, listen, and learn.
2. Being supportive of her opinions and ideas. If you criticize or invalidate her, she'll not reveal her private thoughts.
3. Affirming that you consider all her desires to be perfectly normal. Acknowledge her fantasies.
4. Making her more receptive to your fantasy by assuring her that bisexual desires don't depreciate her value as a lifelong partner. Tell her that diverse fantasies make her more interesting, alluring, and captivating as a sexual partner.
5. Not pushing her into something that scares her. Allow her to become accustomed to the idea. Let her explore the thoughts with you. Women work out their problems by discussing them; encourage her to talk to you.

Use the right words

Females are much more fine-tuned than males when it comes to using the right words. A common mistake males make when attempting to persuade their partners is to use the wrong words, or the right words at the wrong time.

For example, if she fantasizes about having a threesome with a male friend, insensitive guys ask such questions as, "Would you like to suck his cock?" This is a normal thing for a guy to say, but I can assure you that this type of vocabulary is not appreciated by women.

If she mentions that she fancies a threesome with a female friend, an insensitive guy might be silly enough to ask, "Would you like to taste her?" These kinds of comments go too far, too fast, too soon.

In some cases, I know of guys disclosing their fantasies by saying things such as, "I'd like to have sex with two women at once." As you can imagine, this won't go down so well with her. It's always better to say, "I'd like to share you with another woman." This confirms you're not replacing her and she's still the center of your world.

One very important point: When she asks you who that woman would be, your best bet is not to mention any name. Tell her the choice would be hers. This removes any suspicion that you have already done "research" on your project and eases her fear that you want someone she doesn't like. Besides, this will also get her involved in the process.

6

HOW TO PICK AN ENGAGEMENT RING

Moshe Levy, diamond wholesaler

About the Expert: *Moshe Levy has been in the diamond business for ten years. He is the operator of Legend Diamonds in Los Angeles, which wholesales and retails diamonds.*

First of all, you must decide your budget. If you know how much money you would like to spend, that's going to make your life, and the jeweler's, much easier. Once you set your budget, you can start your research.

DeBeers has done research that showed that 60 to 70 percent of brides want to upgrade their stone within the first few years. You don't want to get an engagement ring and put yourself into a hole, and then add to that debt in two years. Get something that you are comfortable with. Then in a year, upgrade to something else you are comfortable with.

Make sure that the store you buy from has an upgrade policy, and get it in writing. Some places tell you that they will give the full amount you paid for a diamond toward the upgrade, but then give you only 50 percent. Make sure you cover yourself.

The diamond is the thing

The main expense is the diamond. The ring is usually a secondary expense. There are a lot of different ways to research and get the information you need. Many resources are online.

Diamonds are divided into a few different categories, and you should decide which one is the most important to you. Some people would say, "I want the biggest, flashiest thing I can get for my money. I don't care about the quality." Others would say, "No, I want the highest quality I can get, even if it is a smaller stone."

Diamonds are categorized by the four "Cs": cut, color, clarity, and carat size. In my opinion, when buying a diamond, the most important thing to look for is the cut. There are certain criteria for the cut.

Cut simply means the way the stone was cut. Sometimes a the person doing the cutting can give you a really good ninety-pointer, and because you want it in a one-carat size, that will give you more for your money in the end than those who choose to cut the stone a little bit heavier, and then you get the one-carat size, but it doesn't look as nice. If you buy a ninety-point or a fifty-point, make sure you get yourself an ideal-cut, or near ideal-cut, stone.

Then you get down to color, clarity, and carat size. You can sacrifice color for better clarity, or you can sacrifice clarity to get a higher color. Hopefully you know the girl you are going to marry fairly well so you can get what she would like.

So you are going to want to know what you want to buy before you even go into the store. Do you want to buy a round stone, a princess-cut diamond, or a marquise diamond?

Clear or huge?

My advice would be to go with a good balance, though it is not a good idea to sacrifice clarity. The bigger the stone, the easier it is to see the inclusions; if you sacrifice clarity and get a bigger stone, you'll be able to see them. My advice? Sacrifice color before clarity.

Always buy a certified diamond. There are a few labs that you can trust: EGL (European Gemological Laboratory), GIA (Gemological Institute of America), and AGS (American Gem Society). It is a very good idea to go to a jeweler or appraiser and make sure the stone is actually the one that is certified. There are a lot of crooks in the diamond business.

Shop around

You want to shop around before buying. You will find that the differences from one store to another will be tremendous. If you live in a big metropolitan area like L.A., New York, Chicago, or Atlanta, or even near one of these areas, it is a really good idea to take a trip to the jewelry districts of these cities.

If you shop there you can probably spend 30 to 40 percent less than at other stores, because that is where the wholesalers are. A lot of the wholesalers have booths, and they sell directly to the public. You still pay tax, but you get a good deal.

Spend as little money as you can on the band. Give her the ring and say, "I didn't know exactly how you wanted the ring to look, so I got a simple band. If you like it, great, but if not we can go and choose the band together."

If your wife-to-be has been specific about the setting, get her what she wants. But if you don't know, or are unsure, get something simple that can be easily replaced.

Know her size

Get her finger size right. You don't want to kneel down and put a ring that doesn't fit onto her finger. To find her size, discreetly borrow one of her rings and take it to a jewelry store. Or go online and order a ring sizer and then, when she is out, size one of her rings. Now when you buy the ring it will be the right size, and when you propose, it will fit on her finger perfectly.

Color costs more

Colored stones are very popular, but they are very expensive because they are rare. Pinks will cost $50,000 to $60,000 per carat. Blues are out of most people's reach—they go for $250,000 to $400,000 per carat. One way to get them without spending too much money is to use colored stones as accent stones in the ring.

7

HOW TO LAST LONGER IN BED

Peter North, adult film star

About the Expert: *One of the leading male adult film stars, Peter North has appeared in hundreds of films including* North Pole #24. *He has appeared alongside adult film stars including Trinity Loren, Christy Canyon, Keisha, Taylor Wayne, Rebecca Wild, Kim McKamy, Jewel De'Nyle, and the legendary—and, at the time, underage—Traci Lords.*

The key to lasting longer is to distract myself but stay in the moment by talking dirty to my girl and telling her to not have an orgasm, which helps me to not have one. It takes my mind off of the physical sensitivity. I'll also move into a new position if I begin to get too sensitive. Yet, I've never tried thinking of something else entirely, like that old adage to "think about baseball."

For men, I recommend desensitizing yourself by having more oral sex. Men have to get through a lot of initial sensitivity to get into what I call "cock shock," where they are still sensitive but not too sensitive—then they can do it for hours.

If you start to get too sensitive you can slow down, and the less verbal your partner is, the easier this is. When you hear how good it feels for your partner, it's hard to not keep pushing forward.

Numbing lotions and penis rings can help, too. They're not dangerous if you follow the manufacturer's instructions.

Take care of yourself

I used to masturbate any time I was going to have sex—but when I did I would get as close as possible, then I would stop and keep myself on the edge by staying as close as possible for about half an hour to get used to holding back. You have to work with it and find what works for you.

Also, stopping the thrusting will help you stave off orgasm. It's best to change the motion to decrease the sensitivity; again, find what works for you. While you're resting, use any form of foreplay on her to keep her going.

You also have to talk with your partner. It's a compliment to your partner to tell her that what she's doing is really working and that you want the experience to last longer. Just tell her—honest and open communication is not only necessary for a great experience, but it can be really sexy.

If you have no problem getting hard after the first erection you might want to just get your first orgasm out of the way because you will last longer the second time. I say have as many as you can!

Find what works

Find what works for you—know which position really works for you and which can help you just maintain a good pace. As long as you and your partner are on the same page, it doesn't really matter—it's more about satisfying each other, so time is not the most important thing. It should never feel like an Olympic event.

8

HOW TO KNOW IF YOUR WIFE
IS CHEATING ON YOU

Paul Dank, owner, Advanced Surveillance Group
and CheatingSpousePI.com

About the Expert: *As owner of Advanced Surveillance Group and CheatingSpousePI.com, Paul Dank has been helping men and women catch their spouses in the act of cheating for many years.*

Our job is to get people proof of what is going on. What we do is work with our clients to try to determine what they suspect is going on, and try to identify any opportunities that we have to catch a cheating spouse in the act.

Usually by the time someone calls us, the suspicions have mounted so much that they think they know, but they just can't prove it. It's not tangible, but all the signs are there. Something is very wrong in the relationship.

It is our experience that cheaters will almost never fess up to cheating unless they are confronted. The reasoning is very simple. If they are having an affair and it's just for the thrill of the sex, then they know that telling their spouse, "Yeah, you know what, I did have an affair and it was because of the thrilling sex," then things at home will never be the same again. If they're having an affair because they love someone else and they want to be with that person, but for whatever reason they can't, then they don't want any more flack than they can handle. They don't want to fess up for that reason, and they want to keep their fallback position intact.

Read the signs

The biggest thing to look for is changes in the spouse's personality. Grooming habits are one example, but it's a long list: change of behavior, weight loss, buying sexy underwear, an unexpected reduction in arguments. Also watch for secretive phone calls. Perhaps they go into the garage to talk on the phone or they go to get milk at nine P.M. and take their phone with them. Maybe the phone bill stops coming to the house, or all of a sudden the phone bill is not itemized. There might be unexplained absences, or absences that were never there before; a lot of overtime but no extra income; ATM withdrawals at strange places.

Watch the office

More than 50 percent of the time the affair is with somebody in the workplace, or somebody who is in the industry. Maybe it's not someone they work with directly, but a colleague at another firm, or a supplier. It could be someone in the office next door.

Gather evidence

How you gather evidence depends on the case. The most common way to do it is through surveillance. We try to determine, as best we can, when that cheating spouse would have an opportunity to be unfaithful. The better job we can do to narrow that down, the quicker we can get the information we need. Determine when and where there will be an opportunity for your spouse to be unfaithful and then put them under surveillance.

There are some areas where we can use vehicle trackers to see where the spouse is going—to see where their actual car is going. Sometimes we do surveillance with one of these devices, which are pretty much GPS devices that show where the car is at all times. However, you can only use them in those jurisdictions where it is legal.

Be very aware of the law. You can't just go around slapping vehicle trackers on cars. However, in many jurisdictions where there is an ownership interest—where both spouses have a right to use the car—you can leave a gym bag containing a tracker in your spouse's car and it's perfectly legal.

Some states specifically prohibit that, but in others it is an excellent tool to use. In Massachusetts it is okay to use a vehicle tracker. In Michigan it is okay to track anybody with a vehicle tracker. (You could slap it on the governor's car because there is not yet a law on the books that prohibits that.) In California using an electronic device of any kind to track somebody's whereabouts is a crime. Each jurisdiction is different; make yourself aware of your local laws before attempting any of these tactics.

Look online

So you think you know everything about your spouse, but little did you know that she has a new identity online, and she's meeting people and doing things you had no idea she was capable of.

Now a lot of people say, "Well, I put her name in Google and I hit return and I didn't find anything about her except her work information." But if you do a very deep Internet search you can locate old documents by cross-referencing any number of things from her past. You can find identities online and try to find out if she is involved in any online communities.

Sometimes you'll find even the silliest things, like she is posting romantic stories, thinking that they are completely anonymous. Internet profiling, as we call it, can be a handy tool if you can spend a lot of time online. Companies like eHarmony are making money hand over fist because people are looking for romantic help online.

Keep notes

Try to document some of what is going on. For instance, say you and your wife were going to meet at home at 5 P.M. and she doesn't show up until 7:45 P.M. and her cell phone was off. She says, "Oh, my gosh, I didn't know it was off. I left you a message. You didn't get my message?" When she does something that doesn't make sense, write it down, and then look for patterns in her behavior.

Try to be objective when you are doing this. When you are going through this, it's very easy to say, "You know what, maybe I am just making this up." That's where you will lose track of all the things that led you to feel the way that you feel. Go with your gut. If you have a true reason to be skeptical of your spouse, don't expect the logical explanation or you will drive yourself crazy.

Like I said before, if they are cheating, they won't tell you they're cheating. If they aren't cheating, they won't tell you they are cheating. So you'll hear either, "I'm not cheating," or "I'm not cheating." You can't believe it either way.

What to avoid

Never, ever mention anything about a private investigator, or threaten to watch your spouse more closely. Once a cheating spouse hears those words, they will modify their behavior, sometimes to the point that they can't be caught.

That's not to say that there aren't people who get scared by that threat and stop what they are doing, but the vast majority will continue. If you go that route, there is absolutely no benefit to making the threat. All you will do is retard your ability to investigate the situation and find the truth.

9

HOW TO CHEAT ON YOUR WIFE

Judith Brandt, author, *The 50-Mile Rule: Your Guide to Infidelity and Extramarital Etiquette*

About the Expert: *Judith E. Brandt wrote* The 50-Mile Rule: Your Guide to Infidelity and Extramarital Etiquette *after waking up one day and questioning why she was married to her husband of seven years. She didn't cheat on him, but after her divorce, she did become "the other woman." That relationship, by turns thrilling, tumultuous, and depressing but always educational, provided the basis for* The 50-Mile Rule.

There are a number of things you have to consider before deciding to cheat. First of all, ultimately, the undiscovered affair is the successful one. Secrecy is essential.

Once the information is out there, once what you are up to is public knowledge, you are entering into a world of hurt. Basically the key to all of this is to keep your affairs secret, because we all know that once anyone knows a secret, it is no longer a secret. Once you understand that, there are some guidelines that you can use to get away with having an affair.

Avoid people you know

First of all, you never want to have an affair within your work or social circles. Follow the fifty-mile rule, i.e., don't have an affair within fifty miles of your house. But you can expand that a little bit—you never want to have an affair within your work or social circles.

The reality is that if you want to keep your affair secret, you have to keep a neutral zone between yourself and the people you run into on a daily basis. You want to keep this between you and people who are not known to your friends or family. Those are probably rules one, two, three, and four in terms of who you pick.

Who to pick

Sometimes the selection just comes to you. You see somebody and say, "Whoa, I'd like to get some of that." Then the process kind of moves on from there.

You should make sure that this is the kind of person who will keep your secret. We all assume when we are in the middle of the affair that the person we are with will love us and is for us so much that even after this affair is over, and even though it may end poorly, that this is someone who will keep our secret. That is a huge assumption.

The reality is that most affairs peter out. They tend to trickle down to some kind of conclusion. Most of the time they don't last indefinitely. I've been involved with a person for fifteen years, but that is unusual. Most of the time affairs wear themselves out in a relatively short amount of time.

You assume that this other person is going to keep this secret close and protect you, but the reality is that that is absolutely not true. When somebody doesn't have an emotional or a financial investment, why should they keep your secret?

Be careful

If you piss somebody off, treat them badly, or don't take their calls, don't think this person is going to say, "Well, he treated me so fabulously for six months, I'll keep his secret." That just isn't the case.

Another thing that people need to be aware of in an affair is that manners count. The way that you behave toward this other person counts. You can't assume that an illicit relationship is going to start at a fever pitch and remain at a fever pitch. Even when you are in it, you need to know in the back of your mind how to end it.

That means what I call being honest but open with the other person. That means you are honest about the fact that maybe you are married with kids, and that you are not going to leave them.

There are other things you shouldn't be honest about. Don't admit, for example, that, "My great wish is to sail around the world." Well, we've all heard some variation of that fantasy. One of the things that is so enticing about affairs and what makes them so attractive is that you have met someone who is really suited to you where you are in your life right now.

Your spouse may see you as a jerk, somebody who tells bad jokes and is never going to get anywhere professionally. So when you go out and have an affair with somebody, it's like getting a clean slate.

Sometimes people are so excited about this fresh start that they begin to divulge every fantasy and every wish that they have. What happens in that situation is that you give away too much. You build an expectation in the affair partner. They begin to say to themselves, "I'll be the person on that sailboat."

If you build up that level of expectation in the other person, when it comes to an end, you are going to be in a lot worse shape than when it began. The affair partner is going to come back and say, "But you said this to me. You said I was going to be the one."

Keep some (not all) things to yourself

You don't want to reveal too much about yourself, simply because all of that information, at some point or another, can be taken and used against you. Men try to get away with not revealing that they are married. You need to be up-front about your status. You don't want somebody to assume that you aren't married when you are.

There are private investigators who are available; there's the Internet. There are all sorts of ways for people to find out who you are, and it is just impossible to keep your life entirely private, so the best advice is to be up-front about that. You don't want to go out of your way to create a fantasy life or a fantasy world because the other person can more easily see themselves taking their place in that fantasy. Do not let the other person have an expectation of you.

Evaluate your risk

Risk evaluation is something that one will find himself doing a lot of when an affair partner presents herself. That is really the sad thing. Affairs are so exhilarating that people should be allowed to enjoy them for what they are, which is often tremendous sexual fulfillment, and even emotional fulfillment sometimes.

There should be so much great sex going on, and you should be allowed to enjoy it. But there is so much other stuff going on in the background, and risk evaluation is part of it. Obviously the risk goes up exponentially when you are sleeping with your sister-in-law, for instance.

One of my favorite stories: A woman who was seeing a guy had a picture of the two of them on her desk. Later on, the wife of the man came into this woman's office on legitimate business and saw the picture and said, "That's my husband." Any man who has his picture taken with the woman he is cheating with is just asking for trouble.

That guy was an idiot. But of course there are so many ways of doing this today. There are now cell phones that take pictures. It's becoming, frankly, more difficult to have a "successful" affair.

So we take a lot of this for granted, that we are in a sense operating in an ancient technological society, when the reality is that we can be found out in a variety of ways. It is possible to get away with it, but you have to be intelligent about it.

When you talk about risk assessment, you need to keep in mind that, for example, there are calling groups that you can contact on the Web that will call your wife and say that you need to be out of town for the weekend. They will actually portray someone from your workplace. They can even produce fake plane tickets and create other smoke screens.

If you get caught

If you get caught, deny, deny, deny. Why? Because your spouse probably doesn't want to know, anyway. When an affair is discovered, all the power shifts to your spouse. She's the one who's going to be making the new rules, whether she decides to stay in the marriage or makes the decision to leave.

Too much comfort

Sometimes people get so comfortable in an affair that they forget it's an affair. They start parading the other person around, or maybe take them to a restaurant that is close to their home. You always want to be conscious that you are in an affair and restrain your urge to brag about this great new girl you have.

Sex

Imagine coming home to your wife and she says, "We've been together now for six years and all of a sudden I've got herpes." Always use condoms—not only to avoid disease, but also to avoid pregnancy.

Should you leave

Second marriages have life cycles—infatuation, attachment, disillusion, and dissolution. One of the things that make mar-

riage so difficult is that the two parties generally—although not always—travel through that life cycle at different rates. If you are at the disillusion stage, reconciling yourself to this marriage will be difficult to say the least.

One doesn't just reverse this cycle. Once the bloom's off it's off, and if you don't have kids or extensive ties to each other, there's little to hold you together except habit and fear.

Part of the reason the life cycle exists is so that people will seek out genetic variety by mating with a variety of people—a desire most of us have that doesn't jibe with law or religious dictate. Nevertheless the desire exists, and the fact that you're attracted to your coworker in much the same way that you originally were to your wife indicates just how accurate a predictor the life cycle can be.

Keep in mind that affairs follow a similar life cycle but the time is greatly compressed. In other words, if your marriage ran the table in four years, your current affair might last only twelve to eighteen months, if that. And if your girlfriend is already getting possessive, you're going to have a whole other set of problems once you're ready to leave.

So, even though you may be done with your marriage for all intents and purposes and think you have found happiness in this new relationship, chances are it's not so. If you decide to divorce, you may just find that you want to put all of this—wife *and* girlfriend—in the past, and start fresh.

Do you want to have to deal with the fallout of your girlfriend's divorce? Deal with her kids if she has any? That's a heavy burden to bear, and once faced with the reality and gravity—not to mention the financial costs—of her situation, you may find that what you feel for her simply isn't enough to balance the aggravation of her divorce.

Or, maybe it will all work. That's one of the tough things about interpersonal relationships: It's hard to know what's right. Staying married may or may not be the right choice for you. There's simply no way to predict that, and no way to

know what the consequences of choosing one way or the other will be. The only way to find out is to make a choice and then live with it.

The bottom line

Love, for better or for worse, is often a crapshoot. If you leave a woman, you may never find anyone you like as much. You may moon over her for the rest of your life. In other words, you may feel down the line like you lost in the love sweepstakes, and maybe you will have.

10

HOW TO BALANCE WORK AND FAMILY

Wayne Parker, professional speaker

About the Expert: *A professional keynote speaker, workshop/seminar facilitator, and organizational consultant, Parker is also the chief administrative officer of the city of Provo, Utah, and served as the management services director for the Ogden City Corporation. Parker has been the city manager of three cities: Smithville, Missouri; Merriam, Kansas; and Roy, Utah. His work contributed to Utah's being designated by* Financial World *magazine as the best-managed state in the United States.*

Men's roles have changed dramatically in the last thirty years. There's a much greater expectation now for men to play significant roles in their families. Fifty years ago, their role was largely that of the breadwinner, and now we have an increase in demand for men to be at home.

And yet, as the workplace has changed over the last fifty years, demands to dedicate more time to work have grown. So, there are now those two pressures working on men at the same time.

To a large extent, balancing work and family is about defining roles and determining what everyone's expectations are. Every family is different, and just about every job is different.

You have to define your role and then set priorities. Trying to juggle a very busy career and a hectic family schedule is difficult, but it is certainly doable.

There are situations in both places in which you can say "No" to the things that are less important and "Yes" to the things that might be more important.

Have priorities

Largely, the balance is a matter of prioritization, of sitting down and taking stock. Decide what is most important at work and what can be delegated. Be careful of accepting assignments, and make sure to define them when they're given. At home, again, what is more important? Where do you want to build the memories with your family?

A lot of us spend too much time creating memories in front of the movie screen or the television. We need to contribute a lot more to personal interaction, creating experiences with our partners and our children that are interactive and transmit our feelings to them. We spend a lot of time in a collective monologue instead of a dialogue.

There are ways to get in touch with your kids or spouse during lunch hour. If you are fortunate enough to work close to home, or from your home, that's great. A lot of families now communicate electronically.

I have a daughter at college three hours away, and we text message at lunchtime periodically just to keep in touch electronically, even though we are physically apart. So I think that there are a variety of things you can do to keep the lines of communication open regardless of how busy you are in your job.

Be honest when job seeking

In my opinion, it is best to be up-front about your family priorities when looking for a job. Because of changes in the law, employers today are not as likely to ask questions about family because it may come across as discriminatory. But I don't think it hurts to let a future employer know that you have a family and that you are committed to them.

As an employer, I would be very interested in people who are committed to family and relationships outside of work. That balance is a positive for an employer. Some shortsighted employers may think, The guy gives me twenty-four hours a day, and I'd like a few extra, but I believe that the wise employers are the ones who recognize that a balanced employee brings a lot to the workplace.

Be balanced

There are stages in life where it seems like diapers and dishes are all that there is. But you realize that in different stages of life, different things become more important. I know that in the early days of my family, with demanding jobs, my wife shouldered more than her share of the responsibilities. We were trying to create opportunities for the family to work together and play together, to set aside some time for a positive experience. Once the kids arrived we realized that the house wasn't always going to be as immaculate as it was before they were born.

Now that our youngest is in junior high school, one of our children is married, and another one is getting married, things are different. It's easier to keep the house clean, and there is a little more focus on positive, interactive relationships with the kids.

Keep things separate

It is tough to keep work and home separate. We live a very integrated lifestyle now. There was a fellow I knew who had a big tree in front of his house and every night when he came home, no matter how bad it was, he sort of symbolically touched a branch on the tree as he walked up to the door. He called it his trouble tree, and it was a place where he could park his troubles from work for the night. That was the psychological tool that he used to leave his worries at the door; then he'd pick them up on his way out the next day.

Try to leave work at work and try to leave home at home. One thing that my wife and I have done for a number of years is take thirty minutes each evening to just sit out on the porch, or take a walk down the block and try to coordinate and talk about what is happening and share some stresses.

It is like a release valve on a pressure cooker. You can communicate every day for that thirty minutes, and it will keep the pressure on the cooker down.

The younger the tougher

It is very tough when you have young children. Our family demands the best from us, and I think in turn, family is where we have to put forth our best effort. The key is understanding what you can live with. Maybe a little clutter at home is acceptable. I think that there are a lot of young dads who don't change their expectations and end up living on the golf course.

Watch the signs

Look for signs. Sense the pressure. Be on the lookout for things like headaches and a stiff neck—those things that we tend to associate with stress. The fuse tends to get a little short when you are experiencing the demands of the daily grind. You watch for the symptoms of stress and anxiety, and then you take the appropriate steps to remove them.

Talk to your kids

One thing my wife and I did with the kids from time to time when they were young was sit down and have a family budgeting session. We did it with Monopoly money. We said, "Okay, here are the resources we have for the family from Mom and Dad's paychecks. Here is where things go—the mortgage, utilities, everything. Now here is what is left."

This helps give kids a feel for what is going on. They can see that maybe the iPod that is high on their list may not be in the family budget. I think it also helps when the kids say, "I want

Mom home more." Well, you can show them that if they want Mom or Dad home more it is going to have a real monetary consequence. Have healthy discussions about financial reality. We started doing this with the kids when they were about five or six years old.

With the major decisions like, "Do we buy an RV? Do we move?" it is healthy to get their input. Again you can bring out the Monopoly money and say, "This is what we need to do this. What can we do, or what can we give up to make this happen?" It all goes back to having open dialogue.

11

HOW TO CARE FOR CHILDREN

Melvin Mora, Baltimore Orioles third baseman
As told to Jerry Beach

About the Expert: *Melvin Mora is the starting third baseman for the Baltimore Orioles and the father of sextuplets.*

Having sextuplets means changing a lot of diapers. At first I didn't know how to do it, so I watched my wife doing it. I saw her holding a baby and changing a diaper. And I knew I had to do it because there was no way she could do it by herself. With six kids, I've had to change as many as forty diapers in one day.

Trial and error

In the beginning it was tough, because they were tiny—they were very tiny and delicate. And you have to clean boys and girls differently.

To clean the girls, you have to go up and down, but with the boys it doesn't matter. These are the things they taught me at the hospital before we brought the kids home.

Once the kids were six or seven months old, I was able to do it really quickly. I was quick changing them—real quick. Once the kids get a little older it does get easier because they stay still. They know when it's time to change diapers. They're quiet and they don't give you a hard time.

As the kids came out of diapers it got a little easier. At first, when it came time to "do potty" in the toilet, some of them wanted to and some of them didn't. They had to get used to it until they learned. During that time they used training pants.

Be involved beyond diapers

I'm always there for my kids, especially when I'm not on the road. I can spend time with them in the morning before I head to the ballpark. I'll do everything I can to try to help my wife—changing diapers, giving the kids milk, taking them to school.

In the afternoon it's tough on my wife because she has to cook for them, she has to change everybody, and she has to give everybody a bath. So when I'm in the house, she has time to spend time with the girls.

Sometimes it's tough, sometimes it's fun. It's tough when they get sick. They get sick, then *everybody* gets sick.

Help and get help

You often need to get help from people who have done it before. Jerry Hairston's wife would always ask my wife if she could help. Buddy Groom's wife would ask me if I needed something when they were tiny and so little. They all helped out.

12

HOW TO GET A DIVORCE

Sam Bradley, divorce attorney

About the Expert: *Sam Bradley is a member of the American Bar Association with a family law practice in Amherst, Ohio.*

When a client comes in wanting a divorce I'll explain to them the types of divorce methods in Ohio. The methods do vary from state to state, but they are similar.

Make sure you are clear on the terminology. For example, in California you get a dissolution of marriage, but here in Ohio we call it a divorce. So it is very important to get an idea of what things are called in your own state.

Types of divorce

You have a dissolution of marriage, which is an agreed-upon divorce. There is the traditional divorce, in which you have a plaintiff suing a defendant and you have to present evidence to a judge, after which the judge determines how things will be divided between the two parties. That doesn't mean that they can't agree upon it at some point and take away the judge's obligation to rule on it.

The third type of "divorce action" is the legal-separation action. That is a support action. At the end of the case you are still married, but each party has an obligation to the support of the other. Again, that is determined by the court. Obviously, one person would be getting support and the other would not. You do not need the other person's agreement to get divorced. In a dissolution action, you would need the agreement because you are agreeing upon things ahead of time. But to simply terminate a marriage, you do not need the other person's consent.

Lots of paperwork

Generally speaking, if you have a dissolution of marriage, you would need a separation agreement. That is pretty much a contract that divides property, determines the responsibility for any children, and informs the world that husband and wife are no longer going to be husband and wife.

Then you attach that contract to what is called a petition for dissolution. The petition gets filed with the court along with that contract and you are scheduled for a hearing. The judge then has to review the contract to make sure that it is full, fair, and equitable. Then, once the court is satisfied that it is, in fact, full, fair, and equitable, the dissolution will be granted.

In a traditional divorce action, where one party sues the other, you need a summons, which is prepared by the clerk's office, and a complaint, which is, for lack of a better word, a complaint for a divorce. In that complaint you would have grounds alleged, or the reasons for divorce. You would probably also have a motion for temporary orders, depending on which side of the case you are on. The whole idea there is to try to get court orders in place to ensure that bills get paid, and to make sure that each party can live reasonably equally. You want to try to avoid having one party economically squeezed.

You don't want to have the moneyed spouse use economic coercion. This type of action will also temporarily divide the children's times between the parents and figure out who is going to be responsible for them on a day-to-day basis. It might also award legal fees to one party or the other.

Another document that is included is the Uniform Child Custody Jurisdiction Enforcement Act affidavit, which aims to prevent parental kidnapping from one state to another. You will also have an application for what is called IV-D Services, which is effectively a federal program for public-assistance benefits.

But in each case, each party is applying for those services and the child support enforcement agency is mandated, by federal law, to assist people in getting support, especially child support. That dates back to the early to mid 1980s, when the whole idea was to shift responsibility from the government back to the parent.

Just get me out

If the parties can't agree upon the value of the house, the lawyer will hire a real-estate appraiser to give an opinion as to what the house would be worth on the market.

Suppose, though, that the wife doesn't agree with the husband's appraiser. She can go out and get her own. Then, at a trial, the judge would hear the testimonies of both experts, and then try to decide which of the two experts seemed more credible. From there, the court would decide who to believe.

The same goes with custody issues. There are a number of factors that the court has a duty to consider in determining custody. These are called the best-interest factors. They are pretty similar from state to state. For the most part, of the two parents, the children will go to the one who will better serve the best interests of the child.

Prenups not always ironclad

In some states, at least, if a prenuptial agreement is entered into very close to the marriage, with only one person having council, there is a good chance that it will be held for naught. Engaged people have a special relationship. The trust level is generally much greater. The courts want to make sure that one party didn't take advantage of the other by using that heavy trust against the weaker person.

Let's say the prenuptial was made properly, that each party fully disclosed everything that they had—debts, assets, everything. Now both parties have an agreement, so it would probably be binding in terms of property. However, the trial court could still—if it addresses spousal support—make a determination that under the present circumstances, it is no longer equitable or fair to require one spouse or the other to live by the terms of their contract because the present incomes were never anticipated.

Be patient

In a dissolution of marriage, the length of time it takes is from the negotiation of the contract of separation to the time of filing. Once it is filed in the courts, the dissolution of marriage has to be completed no earlier than thirty days. That is a statutory cooling-off period—"Maybe they'll get back together." The court loses the right to proceed after ninety days have passed since filing. So there is usually a sixty-day window in which a judge can grant the parties their dissolution. Timelines vary from state to state.

Not much you can do

Truthfully, I don't think that it is possible to be entirely prepared for a divorce. I guess you could be, but you may run into a lot of dishonesty leading up to it because if you are prepping for a divorce, you don't want your spouse to know about it. Again, some spouses never get a chance to prepare, because if one party has prepared, they get blindsided and they may never get sufficient time to prepare for those expenses.

People underestimate the expense: the emotional expense as well as the expense associated with dividing assets and dividing custody of children. There is also the expense associated with having to hire experts, and then the expense of utilizing the lawyers—not a cheap proposition.

13

HOW TO COACH A TEAM

Joe Walton, former head coach of the New York Jets,
current head coach at Robert Morris University

About the Expert: *A legendary football coach with a long
career in the pros, Joe Walton returned to football in 1993 at
Robert Morris University, where he founded the program and
built it into a success. Previously, among his many NFL stops,
Walton served as the head coach of the New York Jets from
1983 to 1989, and his teams achieved a 53-57-1 record.*

The key is getting players who you think will take your instruction and perform the best. From there you have to
get the team's respect. I find that the best way to do that is
through knowledge and fairness. You also want to be consis-
tent with all of your decisions.

One of the key things in coaching is using drills—practice
sessions as close to game situations as you can get. There are a
lot of coaches who do a lot of things in practice that they are
not going to do in the game. You want all your drills and all
your practices to be close to game situations. The way the players react in practice is the way they are going to react in the
game. Be in a constant state of preparing.

You also want to constantly evaluate your talent. We are
constantly evaluating in training camp. Every night the coaches
rate, by position, who they think the best players are. In training camp, we have everything all planned out before we go to
camp: what we are going to do in the meetings at night; what
part of the system is going to be put in. Then we make practice schedules for every day to make sure that we cover everything in our individual drills and in our seven-on-sevens and

those types of things. Everything is scheduled and planned before we go to camp.

Training camp, or two-a-days, or whatever you want to call the practices that lead up to the season, are critical for teaching. This is when you have to get everyone on the same page and see where you stand. We work on a combination of fundamental drills and installing plays. We'll have the individual positions work on their techniques, then come together as an offense and a defense to install our systems.

Get good players

Even the best players sometimes slip through the cracks. For every blue-chip star who signs with a prestigious school, a truly capable athlete finds himself having to "walk on" to the team. The key is to find that diamond in the rough.

We subscribe to several scouting services that provide us with the names and accomplishments of athletes from across the country. The same can be applied in smaller situations, only *you* have to be the judge of the talent.

Once you get your team together you have to make some tough decisions and begin the teaching process.

Coach, practice, repeat

You have to keep installing. Some kids fall behind, so try not only to put in something new every day, but keep reviewing every day. In other words, if I put three 40 passes in tonight for tomorrow, then the next night I have to put some of the other passes in. So that next day we'll work on those new passes, but also go over the ones from the previous day. Eventually it starts to set in for the team.

It's all about repetition. The more times you run a particular play in practice, the better it will run when it counts—in a game. There was a game we won on the last play that was set up by what we call a "clever play." It was a hook and lateral that timed up just right for us. After the game I explained that we practice that play every week. Some of the reporters asked why we would practice a play like that every week. I told them, "Because we might need it."

You want everyone on the team, including the coaching staff, to be on the same page. Coaching is just like teaching. It's educating the players about the game and getting the most out of their abilities.

No hitting in practice

No hitting in practice—that comes from my days in the NFL. We usually saved all the hitting for Sundays, but there is another reason for this rule as well. Over the years I've been here, I've found that you don't get a lot of great players. I mean, you'll get core of about twenty-two or thirty. You can't take too many injuries, which holds true at lower levels as well as the NFL.

You don't have the backups that you might have in pro football, or you can't pick up a guy on waivers like you can in pro football. You're stuck with what you've got. So I've concentrated on learning, teaching, drilling, and making sure that they understand the game plan, and then I let them hit on Saturday.

We always work on fundamentals. I've never changed that since I became a head coach. About the only difference between here and the pros is that I use more time at the beginning of practice going over the game plan.

The reason is that we don't have as much time for meetings in college as we did in pro ball. We have to work around class schedules, so we try to have extra meetings on the practice field.

Practice begins with a lap around the practice field and a stretching session. From there the individual positions split up for fundamental work with their position coaches. Receivers work on routes and on catching the ball. Offensive linemen work on releases and blocking techniques.

Everyone is working on their aspect of the game. It isn't

until later that we come together as an offensive and defensive unit to put in our plays. We want to make sure that everyone knows where he is supposed to be on the field and when he is supposed to be there so that we can have our best shot at success. We'll line up and walk through what each player is going to do on that play, and what changes we have to make in regard to an opponent's tendencies.

Once we've gone over everything, we'll have a little live scrimmage time. But, again, there is no tackling. Everything is full-speed at this point, but we don't want any of our people to get hurt, so no one is to be on the ground.

Be flexible

I believe that a big part of coaching is recognizing talent. We'll move someone to tight end, or we'll move someone to defensive back to try to get our best players on the field. It's kind of silly to have four receivers who can run and play well and use only three of them.

Sometimes what we might do is use one of them to play defensive back, because he may have good agility, good speed, and good hands. So I think that one of the challenges of football outside of the pros is to get your best football players out on the field. You don't want them sitting on the bench.

Have a thick skin

No doubt about it, no matter where you coach, you need a thick skin. There is a lot of second-guessing in every sport. In baseball, it's always, "Why'd you take the pitcher out?" Once you take him out, it's, "Why'd you leave him in so long?"

You gotta do what you believe. You gotta do what you practice and what you studied, and hope for the best.

While the average person may have to make only a handful of really tough decisions in a lifetime, a head coach faces countless decisions every week that will impact the outcome of a game and ultimately the careers of his staff and players. Win the game and you're a hero.

You have to weigh the level of risk against the level of potential reward. You're not going to go for it in a fourth and 23 situation, but you might if it were fourth and 2.

Many people make decisions without really thinking through all the possible consequences. They see one potential reward and gamble their livelihood and the livelihoods of others without careful consideration. You know that by benching a player, he will be hurt. But if he isn't playing well and you have someone who can take his place, the entire team will be better off for the substitution.

Weigh the needs of many against the needs of a few. You should also prepare to make a sacrifice in order to make a good decision. You'll be questioned. There will be people who don't agree with the way you'll do something, and you'll have to hear about it. But that is part of making those big decisions. You have to be able to take the heat.

How to Get an Athletic Scholarship

During the peak of the high school recruiting season, many athletes of varying levels of talent get bombarded with letters from colleges and universities containing questionnaires. Even if your child may not be particularly interested in that school, fill out the form and send it back.

We send out tons of those things. We just ship them out all over and hope to get a good response. It really helps us, because you can't get out to every high school game to scout players. This brings the players to us.

A relatively new component of the college recruiting process is the recruiting night. High schools and high school athletic conferences have started putting these on. We'll send a coach and he will spend the night talking with all the coaches from that conference. They all have videotapes and write-ups on their players.

Schools and conferences also organize combines. They invite college coaches to come and watch high school athletes go through a series of drills including the forty-yard dash and vertical jumps. The athletes who attend these combines get a leg up on those who do not.

Parents of athletes who may not have access to these tools can take matters into their own hands and send a homemade "highlight film" to any number of schools. Make a tape, write a letter, and send it in. It's tough to find those guys who play for small schools in remote areas.

Look for a school or program that is developing, or rebuilding. While it may not be the most glamorous thing to get a scholarship to Eastern Michigan University, your child will still end up with a free college education and a better chance of seeing the field than he would at Ohio State.

Anyone we're in competition with gives scholarships, and it can get really competitive. A lot of times we'll try to find the guys who are overlooked. That was how we came across Tim Hall. Tim was a standout running back from Kemper Military Academy. Not heavily recruited out of high school, Hall attended Kemper in part to further his athletic career. After two years at the junior college, Hall enrolled at Robert Morris. Once we got him into our system he flourished and was eventually drafted by the Oakland Raiders in the sixth round of the NFL draft. He went on to have a successful career with the Raiders.

While following these tips will get your child on the radar screen of countless college coaches, the single biggest factor in landing the elusive college scholarship rests solely on the shoulders of the student athletes themselves. Work hard and play well in high school.

Top Ten Keys to Getting Noticed by a College Coach

1. Work hard and play well in high school.
2. Get your name out there.
3. Fill out school-sanctioned questionnaires.
4. Attend combines.
5. Organize a recruiting night.
6. Make a highlight film and send it out.

7. Attend college athletic camps.
8. Look for programs "on the rise."
9. Specialize in a specific component of the game, e.g., holding for field goals.
10. Work the phones.

14

HOW TO GET A JOB IN SPORTS

Bill Dwyre, sports editor, the *Los Angeles Times*

About the Expert: *Bill Dwyre is sports editor of the* Los Angeles Times. *He appears on a variety of local and national talk shows speaking about sports topics.*

In one way, finding a job in sports is like finding a job in any other field—getting in the door is key. There are countless people who want to work in sports, but only some of them will take the steps necessary to fight their way inside the profession. If you want to make your living in sports, you will most likely have to start from the bottom and show that you are willing to make the sacrifices needed to succeed.

Degree of difficulty

Getting a college degree is not absolutely necessary, but it is a great first step toward breaking into sports. If you are going to go down that path you'll want to get your degree in journalism, marketing, or a field that relates to what you ultimately want to do.

Still, in most cases, some degree is better than no degree, so a liberal arts or an English degree would be fine. Going to college also helps because you have an athletic department right on campus that you could work for, and most schools have a newspaper where you can begin to amass some clips covering the school's teams.

If you do go to school, however, you should make sure you take advantage of the mistakes other students will make. The biggest thing to avoid is doing the yuppie thing and not using your vacations, breaks, and time after graduation well. Use this time to gain experience as an intern or in on-campus jobs, or to get a leg up on the competition. Don't go out right after graduation and take a vacation. Get out there and get your feet wet.

Whether or not you go to school, the most important skill for nearly every career in sports other than professional athlete is writing. If you want to be a journalist or work in sales or marketing for a team, or have dreams of being in player personnel, you will need to be able to put pen to paper.

Humble beginnings

Sports is not a nine-to-five field, and there is no entry-level job that's relatively easy for anyone to get. Treating a potential career around athletes like any other profession will leave you stuck on the outside.

Getting your start usually requires taking an internship—a low-paying or unpaid job at the absolute bottom rung of the industry. But, like I said, getting your foot in the door is crucial. Volunteer if you have to. Do whatever you can to get in the door and show them what you can do. If you're serious about this as a career, all you need is an opportunity to show you belong.

Most professional sports leagues have internship programs. These jobs are in high demand, however, and can be hard to obtain. In some ways, setting your sights on an internship a little farther down the ladder can be better because it has a better chance of leading to a job.

College—specifically your college, if you attended one—can be a great place to look. Most sports information offices (the public relations department for a college's athletics program) and athletic director's offices are looking for help. Although they may not start you working with the basketball team or any of the other marquee sports, there is almost always a need for work with the less popular teams.

Get your start promoting the water polo team and do the best job that anyone has ever done. Put in long hours, be creative, and show that you are willing to do whatever it takes. Just get your foot in the door, show that you belong, and when there's an opening in the department, you will be on the short list to fill it.

When starting your job search, also remember the people who might be able to help you. Whether it's a player on a college team you covered who made it to the pros, someone you met in school, or an old family friend, any angle can help.

Connections, like with any other job, can be a big help. But if you are completely new and know absolutely nobody, just be a little better and a little more driven than the next guy.

TV or not TV

Today television sets the agenda because of the fast-moving nature of sports. So, if you're young and eager, there are dozens of producers who are looking for you. With the proliferation of cable channels, there is an almost bottomless need for programming.

Newspapers have a limit for writers and space. TV is almost infinite. There are so many hours of programming, and stations are looking for young, ambitious people to help fill them (and to work the long, thankless hours required to do so).

The downside to the many opportunities being offered in television is the unstable nature of the industry. Newspapers never get cancelled, but TV jobs can go away quickly. If you want stability, look into print media. If you want fast-paced, get into TV.

One area I'd steer people away from is sports talk radio, but that is just a personal thing. I'm convinced that sports talk radio is a sign of the apocalypse. Where else can "Jerry" from Van Nuys become a celebrity after he has slandered five people in his first sentence?

Feed the beast

Guys are going so fast and creating so much junk that we need to feed the beast, and that creates jobs. If you're worried about these types of jobs being eliminated, just take a look at the last baseball strike. People were saying, "We're never going back," but attendance keeps going up.

Audiences keep growing and people keep discovering sports. That keeps a new readership coming in almost perpetually. Just look at what ESPN has done with the X-Games. I'm an old cynic, but that is a whole genre of "sports" that has sprung up out of nowhere. Twenty years ago newspapers weren't covering skateboarding events, but now it's national news.

That is how powerful TV is now. Things that weren't sports twenty years ago are all of a sudden. It has changed the way we run things here because now I have to send someone to cover these events, when before they were ignored by the media, and this was accepted.

Youth sports are all driven by television. TV now creates a genre and, once it has, the media then has to cover it. The same can be said for "made-for-TV" events. Tiger Woods playing someone one-on-one on prime-time television isn't a PGA Tournament, but, as a newspaper, we had better have the people to cover it because people want to read about it. It is just another example of how TV dictates what is news. I may not like it, but it's good for job seekers.

No magic bullet

The next generation of sports professionals is no different from any other generation. If you're good and bright and you care about the subject matter you'll do fine. If you set your jaw and do it every day, you'll find that you can get just about any job you want in sports.

15

HOW TO THROW A PERFECT SPIRAL

Bernie Kosar, former Cleveland Browns quarterback

About the Expert: *Bernie Kosar played for the Cleveland Browns for most of his career before finishing his playing days as a backup for the Miami Dolphins and Dallas Cowboys.*

If you start thinking about the mechanics of throwing the ball too much, you are going to get into trouble. Earl Moore, my coach at the University of Miami, used to tell us not to think too much. But throwing a good spiral is still very important. It makes it easier to hit your receivers, and it also makes it easier for them to catch.

One of the first things you need to consider before throwing the ball is the weather conditions. Believe it or not, the biggest thing that will disrupt a pass is the wind—not the rain, snow, heat, or mud.

You need good mechanics

A big part of throwing a football is getting the feel for it. You can tinker with this and tinker with that, but if you don't have a feel for the ball, it won't go where you want it to go.

If you look at my old films you'll see that I had a lot of flaws in my delivery, but there are a couple of things that you want to do in terms of gripping the ball. Earl used to count the number of fingers we had on the laces. Some guys had three or four fingers on them. I had one. Terry Bradshaw had none. You have to have very big hands to do that. You also want to have a cup on the bottom of the ball. There has to be some space between your palm and the ball. You don't want your hand to be flat.

During the delivery, as your arm comes forward, your hand should be snapping outward. If you've seen a baseball pitcher throw a curveball, you'll notice that when he's completed the pitch, his palm is facing his body. It is just the opposite when throwing a football: You want to "spin" or "snap" the ball so that your palm is facing outward, away from your body.

Your legs are also very important in throwing the ball. You want to have a good base under you when throwing. So if you are taking a drop, or just playing catch, you want your legs under you. In a perfect world, you want to throw off of your back leg, transferring your weight to the front leg as your arm moves forward. But if you are in a game and five huge monsters are coming at you, you've got to get that thing out of your hands any way you can.

There are so many different things that can impact your throw and keep you from throwing off of your back foot. There are zone-blitzes and all sorts of defensive schemes. I'd love to just chill in a seven-on-seven and chuck it up there all day, but that isn't going to happen. You just have to get your feet under you as best as you can and try to make a good throw.

Things to avoid

There is one thing that has come up more recently that is messing up a lot of young quarterbacks. I was taught in the old school, under guys like Don Shula, and how they taught quarterbacks to throw was to work on the longer passes and then make your way down to the shorter ones.

Now, with the West Coast Offense being so big, guys are looking to the shorter passes and then going right to their check-downs. That hurts them when they have to throw deep, because they can't get the timing down. Once you can throw the deep ball, it becomes easier to hit those short and intermediate passes.

Hitting a moving target

You want to lead your receiver, but not too much. That is all just working with the guy and knowing how he runs routes. Once you get into a game, you have to be able to know where the man coverage is, and where the mismatch is. Then, because you have worked with the receiver and know how much to lead him, you'll hit that deep pass.

16

HOW TO PLAY NO-LIMIT TEXAS HOLD 'EM

Amarillo Slim, poker legend

About the Expert: *Amarillo Slim won the World Series of Poker in 1972, appeared on* The Tonight Show *eleven times, and is considered one of the greatest poker players to ever live. Among his most famous bets, Slim beat Minnesota Fats playing pool with a broom and Evel Knievel in golf with a carpenter's hammer. He took Willie Nelson for $300,000 playing dominoes; Bobby Riggs for $100,000 playing Ping-Pong (with a skillet!); and Bob Stupak for $65,000 pitching coins. His memoir is titled* Amarillo Slim in a World Full of Fat People.

For all major poker tournaments, the betting is no-limit, meaning you can bet anything that's in front of you at any time, or pot-limit, meaning you can bet the amount of the pot at any time. Real poker players, like those who reside in Texas, consider no-limit the only way to play.

Now don't get me wrong, limit poker can be a lot of fun— if you haven't got the guts of an earthworm or if you make your living as an accountant. As far as I'm concerned, if you can't move all in on someone, meaning bet everything you've got in front of you, then it's not real poker.

So, naturally, No-Limit Texas Hold 'em is my game of choice, and it's what is played to determine the winner of the World Series of Poker, where a fella won $5 million for first place in 2004. Now that's a mound of chips that a showdog couldn't jump over and made the $80,000 I got for winning in 1972 seem like chicken feed.

In Hold 'em, each player is dealt two cards facedown, followed by a round of betting. Then, three cards are "flopped" in the middle of the table, faceup, and there's a second round of betting. These are "community cards" that every player can use with the two cards he has to make a hand. Then, a fourth card is turned faceup in the middle, followed by the third round of betting. Last, the fifth card is dealt faceup; this card is called the river—and let me tell you, partner, many a man has been drowned there—followed by the fourth and final round of betting. With the two cards in your hand and the five community cards, you've got to make your best five-card hand.

That's the only part I can teach you, because winning is less about the cards and more about the people. This list should at least get you to break even.

Amarillo Slim's Top Ten Keys to No-Limit Texas Hold 'em

1. Play the players more than you play the cards.
2. Choose the right opponents. If you don't see a sucker at the table, you're it.
3. Never play with money you can't afford to lose.
4. Be tight and aggressive; don't play many hands, but when you do, be prepared to move in.
5. Always be observant at a poker game. The minute you're there, you're working.
6. Watch the other players for "tells" before you look at your own cards.
7. Diversify your play so other players can't pick up tells on you.
8. Choose your speed based on the direction of the game. Play slow in a fast game and fast in a slow game.
9. Be able to quit a loser and, for goodness' sake, keep playing when you're winning.
10. Conduct yourself honorably so you're always invited back.

If you can master the first item on that list, it's the only thing you'll ever need: Play the *players* more than you play the *cards*.

What they say is true: A man's eyes mirror his soul. Why do you think I always wear a big-old brimmed Stetson when I play? A man's eyes show 90 percent of what he's thinking. When I'm wearing my hat, you can only see my eyes when I want you to.

How to Spot a Tell

Besides what you can see from a person's eyes, you also can pick up something about his hand from other physical giveaways, which we old-timers call "tells."

The word "tell" comes from the word "telegraph," meaning to give away or make obvious. In poker, a tell gives away information about a player's hand. In the movie *Rounders*, Mike (Matt Damon) detects a tell from Teddy KGB (John Malkovich) based on the way he eats Oreo cookies. Something as subtle as the way a player sits in his chair or throws his chips in the pot may give you an indication of the player's hand.

Go to any card room and watch a high-stakes poker game. Study a professional player and you'll notice that when the cards are dealt, he watches his opponents to see their immediate reactions before he bothers to look at his own cards. If an opponent winces in disgust when he looks at his cards, the pro has picked up a valuable tell and knows that he can bet and win the pot—whether he has a good hand or not.

One player may talk a lot if he's got a hand, giving signs of being anxious to raise, while another player may become very quiet if he's holding something. The late Jack "Treetop" Strauss, a world-class player who won the World Series in 1982, whistled ever so quietly when he was bluffing. Shoot, neighbor, if you can pick up a tell like that on somebody, he might was well be playing with his hand faceup.

Jimmy Chagra wasn't the type of man you wanted to associate with, but it was hard not to gamble with him. A cocaine dealer who went through millions like most people go through toilet paper, Chagra came to Vegas for his last hurrah while awaiting trial in Texas. Chagra always wanted to beat me at something, so after I had fleeced him on the golf course and at the poker table enough times, he got a hold of Betty Carey to play me in a head-up poker game at the Las Vegas Hilton.

Betty, an attractive woman from Cody, Wyoming, was the most aggressive player I'd ever played against. She was also regarded as the best woman player in the world, and there ain't no question she was. Jimmy staked her $100,000 to play me head-up in a No-Limit Texas Hold 'em freeze-out, which is our word for "winner takes all."

We sat down to play and gave our money to the floor man, who went to get our chips. Betty and I were just sitting at the table with the dealer and the hangers-on, who were sucking around the rail and waiting for old Slim to get shown up by a nice little lady.

I was drinking coffee, which I usually did when I played, and I said, "Betty, I'm gonna have some more coffee. Would you like some?"

"No, thank you, Slim," she said, "but I will have some hot tea."

I wasn't thinking anything of it at the time, about how she said it, but as a poker player, you're *always* working, trying to learn just the smallest thing about an opponent that might make the difference in a big pot. Well, it took a while to get the cards and count out $200,000 worth of chips, and I finished my coffee, and just real casual, I asked, "Betty, how is your tea?"

"Oh, wonderful," she said. "This is real good tea."

And I knew she liked it. She had no reason to lie; it wasn't like she needed to convince me that the tea at the Las Vegas Hilton was just as good as the Queen Mother's. She could have been drinking rat piss as far as I was concerned, but the way she said she liked that tea, that got me to thinking. So I thought, Well, after a while I'll ask her something else, and see how she answers.

About an hour later, a big pot came up—one that was so big a show dog couldn't jump over it—and she moved in on me. Here she was risking all her chips, and I smelled a bluff. I just didn't think she had anything, so just like we were having a normal conversation, I said to her, "Betty, how do you like your hand?"

"Real good hand, Slim," she said, but the tone of her voice was just a little bit different than when I had asked her about the tea. It lacked the same sincerity. Now I knew she was lying! I knew that her answer about the tea was sincere, and this one wasn't. So I called her with a lousy pair of fives, and I won the pot. She didn't disappoint me one bit; she had nothing and had been making a stone-cold bluff.

After I won, I bragged to everyone there that a woman would have a better chance of putting a wildcat in a tobacco sack than she would of beating me at poker.

Of course that only made Betty want to beat me more, and the next time I played her, again it was a $100,000 freeze-out, but Jimmy staked her on the condition that she wear earplugs. Boy, that was hard—talking to my opponents is my secret weapon, and I couldn't get much of a read on her or pick up any tells from her voice. Sure enough, she busted my skinny ass and made me eat my words.

17

HOW TO WIN MORE (OR LOSE LESS) AT A CASINO

Bill Burton, gambling expert, About.com casino gambling host

About the Expert: *Bill Burton is the author of* Get the Edge at Low-Limit Texas Hold 'Em *and is About.com's casino gambling host.*

As far as casino games go, one of the best to play is blackjack. If you play basic strategy in blackjack, you can cut the house edge down to half of a percent. If you learn how to count cards, you can actually get an edge.

Despite what many people think, counting cards is not illegal. You are using your brain. The problem is that casinos in Las Vegas will bar you if they catch you doing it. They'll come up and tap you on the shoulder and say, "Your game is too strong for us, and you can't play blackjack again."

In Atlantic City they cannot throw you out of a casino. There was a lawsuit filed there regarding card counters, so now they can't bar them. But what they can do now is tell you that you have to flat bet, say, ten dollars, or that you can't bet more than twenty-five dollars. They will also shuffle up on you.

Buy a guide

I recommend picking up a basic blackjack strategy guide. There is also software out there that allows you to practice. You can actually bring a basic strategy chart with you to the table; you can walk right in with it. Sometimes the pit bosses, because they know basic strategy so they can spot card counters, will tell you, "Geez, you didn't play that correctly." So many people know basic strategy that if you are sitting at the table and you make a move counter to basic strategy, people will look at you, and in some instances will even yell at you.

Basic strategy comprises the mathematically best times to do certain things. It informs you when to hit, when to stand, and when to double-down in every situation based on the dealer's up card and the two cards in your hand. Some examples: Always double down on eleven; never split fives; split your aces and eights.

Know when to hold 'em

You can actually have an advantage in any poker game. Poker is a game where you can actually have an advantage because you are not playing against the house; you are playing against other players. It is one of those games where the knowledgeable player will win money in the long run and the person without skill will lose.

When you sit down and play at the casino, or you play on-line, probably 80 to 90 percent of the people who sit in the low-limit game have never read a book about the game. Most of them don't know how to play, and that is where you can get your advantage.

Texas Hold 'em looks so simple, but it is actually a little complicated. People think that any two cards can win. Texas Hold 'em is also a positional game. In other words, where you are in relation to the dealer button is important.

If you are the first one to act after the blinds, you need a stronger hand than somebody sitting just to the left of the button or on the button, because once you enter the pot it can be raised and reraised. All of a sudden you find yourself involved in the hand, and it will cost you if you don't have very strong cards.

Whereas when you are in a later position, you already know what most of the table has done. It allows you to play some hands that maybe you wouldn't normally play in an early position. That is another concept that most novice players don't even take into account.

What to play

After blackjack, craps is the best bet for a table game. Your pass line bet in craps only has a 1.41 percent house edge. And placing your six and your eight only has about a 1.5 percent edge. Those are the best bets in the casinos.

Most new games like Let It Ride and Caribbean stud only fall to about 3 percent. The only caveat there is never, ever play the side bets. Those are where you put a dollar down and, like in Caribbean stud, you can win the progressive jackpot. Most of those side bets have a high house edge like 14 to 16 percent, based on what the payout is. Most of the side bets are sucker bets.

Slots, in my opinion, are not worth it. But let me backtrack. It really depends on where you are. In Connecticut and in Atlantic City with the quarter slot machines, the house edge is probably about 8 percent. You go to Las Vegas, and there are some slots that are 99 percent payback. That is just to keep the gamblers in the casino. Keep in mind that those are not the only slots in the house.

The one thing with video poker (and I don't consider that a slot game even though it is a machine game) is that based on the pay table, you can actually tell what the payback for each hand is on that particular game. This is because it is based on a fifty-two-card deck, or a fifty-three-card deck if jokers are involved, so the mathematical probability of making any hand is known.

The way that they adjust the house edge on video poker is to change the pay table. In other words, a full pay jacks-or-better machine will pay nine coins for the full house, six coins for the flush, and two coins for a two pair. Based on most of the tables that machine will pay back 99.5 percent, so it is almost as good as blackjack.

In Connecticut the full house pays six coins and the flush

pays five coins and that cuts the payback to about 94 percent. So just by adjusting what they are paying back makes a big 5 percent difference. But most of the slots in Connecticut and Atlantic City are about 8 percent, which is an awful lot to give back to the house.

Have a budget

I am a big proponent of money management. Whenever you go into a casino, look at it as entertainment. Say, "I'm going to risk a hundred dollars for entertainment and when it's gone, it's gone."

And if you are going to be there for a while, like a three-day vacation in Las Vegas, plan ahead. Take, say, $900 to gamble. Divide that $900 so that you have $300 a day with which to gamble. If you're going to gamble three times a day, break that $300 down again, to $100 per session. That way you always know, whenever you sit down at that table, the maximum that you are going to lose.

Leave the credit cards at home. Never play on borrowed money. Look at it as if you were going camping: You wouldn't eat all your food in one day; if you are going on a gambling vacation, you don't want to use your whole bankroll in one day.

Keep your winnings

Take all the money you won in a single day, the $300 you started with and your winnings, put it all in a sealed envelope, and put it in the safe. The next day, start with the next $300. If you have a winning day one day and a losing day the next, chances are you can still bring something home with you.

Now if you are at the table and you are ahead, I recommend taking half of your winnings and your initial buy-in and playing with the other half of your winnings. The problem that most people have when they find themselves up is that they say, "Well, I'm playing with the house's money."

That is not right because once you win it, it belongs to you. It's your money.

Luck versus skill

The traditional games of skill are blackjack and poker. It is now being found out that with craps, people are learning how to control the dice throw, throwing the dice with same motion and timing to avoid the seven. Even games like Let It Ride have a basic strategy to them. Roulette and slot machines, on the other hand, are all luck. And if you are a player who doesn't know about the game you are playing, you are dependent on luck.

Learn all you can about the game that you want to play. You can find books and tons of material on the Internet, or use computer software to learn to play.

It is all based on math. Those big mega-resorts weren't built on luck. That is why they don't sweat it when someone sits down at the craps or the blackjack table and has a run of luck. They are open 24-7, and they know that in the long run the math of the game will work out in their favor.

In fact, casinos would prefer if everybody who walked in the casino the first time had a wining session. Because that is how you get hooked. So many people have said after a big day at the casino, "Oh, this is easy, I'm going to do this for a living."

There is a house edge to everything. You are there for entertainment. If you are lucky enough to win, you have to have the discipline to put that money aside. You also have to have realistic expectations. You are not going to sit down with $100 and run it up to $100,000. If you start with $100 and you win $25, you've just made 25 percent on your investment. You wish your mutual fund did as well.

18

HOW TO BET AT THE TRACK

Jerry Bailey, Racing Hall of Fame jockey

About the Expert: *Jerry Bailey won the Eclipse Award as the nation's best jockey seven times between 1997 and 2005. He has won the Kentucky Derby, the Preakness, and the Belmont Stakes twice each, has won a record fourteen Breeders' Cup races, and in 1995 was inducted into the Racing Hall of Fame.*

People who have no idea what they are doing shouldn't expect to win. You should allow a certain amount of money to have fun. If you win, great. If you don't, don't be too disappointed. And don't bet more than you can afford to lose.

If you don't want to read *The Racing Form* regularly to gain important racing knowledge, just simply bet on a name that sounds good to you. Pick a favorite number. Bet on the jockey, or the trainer, or a combination of the two that have the highest winning percentage. Or if you know a famous jockey or trainer, you can stick with him.

Who's your daddy?

If you're familiar with the mother or father of a horse, whose names are given in the racing program, you can bet based on lineage.

Before the race, go down and look at the horse. Look at him in the saddling enclosure before the jockeys come out. See what the horse looks like. A lot of times the horse will run well based on appearance. If you are trying to narrow it down between several good-looking horses in one race, if one seems overly sweaty, that is a bad sign. You can sometimes eliminate that horse.

And if you are dealing with grass racing—some races are run on grass, some are run on dirt—look for a horse with a big, flat foot, which is typically good for grass racing.

What bets to place

It is hard enough trying to pick a horse to win, but it is even harder to win the more complicated bets. They pay more, so the degree of difficulty is higher, but the reward is also greater.

A lot of racetracks have rotating pick threes. So you can pick any three in consecutive races and try to pick the winner in each race, like the fourth, fifth, sixth; or the fifth, sixth, seventh; or the sixth, seventh, eighth. Those typically have a bigger payout. Daily doubles are also good races. If you really like the appearance or the form of a horse in the first race, you can single him out and pick several horses in the second race to attach to that horse.

Reading the jockey

Typically the jockey is only about 10 percent of the outcome. A great jockey can't make a bad horse win, but a bad jockey can get a good horse beat.

I would recommend watching the jockeys come out. There are certain tracks where you can watch jockeys weigh in.

Watch the horse's saddle and watch what goes on in the saddling paddock. There are few tracks that will allow you on the trackside. But a lot of the races start and finish in front of the grandstand. If you can, go down to the trackside, instead of sitting in the grandstand, and experience the gate atmosphere, the loading, and the excitement of the actual start.

Downtime

In between races, when you go down and look at the horses in the saddling enclosure, is called downtime. Once the race is over the jockeys go in. Then, if you are lucky, you can go and cash your ticket. If not, make your way to the saddling paddock—that is where the horses for the next race are coming in. That is typically how it goes.

What races to watch

The Triple Crown Races are unbelievable. Saratoga and Delmar are two of the coolest places you can go: Saratoga for the east coast, from the last week in July to Labor Day, you can actually talk to the jockeys on their way to the paddock and on the way back after the race. They will stop and you can get autographs. Delmar is not quite as hands-on, but it is still a cool place for people on the west coast.

Menu of Bets

WIN: You bet on a horse to finish first.

PLACE: Your horse must finish first or second.

SHOW: Your horse must finish first, second, or third.

ACROSS THE BOARD: You're betting win, place, *and* show. If your horse wins, you collect on the win, place, and show bets. If your horse comes in second, you collect on the place and show bets; in third, you collect on the show bet.

DAILY DOUBLE: Pick the winners of the first and second races. Hard, but the payoff is sweet.

QUINELLA: Pick the horses that come in first and second in a race in *any* order.

EXACTA: Pick the horses that come in first and second in a race in the *exact* order.

TRIFECTA: Pick the first three finishers of a race in *exact* order.

SUPERFECTA: Pick the first four finishers of a race in *exact* order.

PICK THREE: Pick the winners of three races in a row.

PICK SIX: Pick the winners of six consecutive races.

BOX: If you have two or more horses that you think will finish in the top spots, but are not sure of the order, you can box them.

WHEEL: A bet on one horse with *all* the others in the race. An "Exacta wheel #5–all" wins if the #5 horse wins and *any* horse comes in second.

KEY OR PART WHEEL: A bet on one horse with *some* of the others. An "Exacta wheel #5–2,3,4" wins if the #5 horse wins and either the #2, #3, or #4 horse comes in second.

—Courtesy of the National Thoroughbred Racing Association

19

HOW TO IMPROVE YOUR GOLF GAME

Mark Blakemore, PGA golf professional

About the Expert: *Mark Blakemore is a PGA golf professional teaching at Boundary Oak Golf Course in Walnut Creek, California, and at Roddy Ranch Golf Clubs in Antioch, California. He is a PGA Class A professional with over twenty years of golf instruction experience. He is also a two-time finalist National Long Driving Champion and a former West Coast Long Drive Champion, and he has a master's degree (Biomechanics/Exercise Physiology).*

Lessons are a must for anyone who wants to improve his or her game. Golf is not the kind of game that you can just play. For example, I was talking with a guy who was a high school quarterback and considered himself to be a very good natural athlete, and he was having trouble improving his golf despite playing for several years. He just wasn't getting any better.

Golf is not the kind of game for which you can use raw, natural athletic ability to overcome shortfalls. It is more refined than that. There is a lot of technique involved; improving your game is a long-term project.

Since there is so much refinement involved in golf, people can't generally teach themselves the game. You will need some kind of instruction, some kind of input in the kinds of adjustments you will have to make.

The bottom line generally is that your movements have to be less complicated. What most people do, by instinct, is almost invariably wrong. A lot of it is counterintuitive at first. Get some kind of input first, because it is going to take practice, whether you have good technique or not.

One thing at a time

The list of things that you need to achieve to have a decent golf swing is very, very long. It's best to do it one action at a time. Then, the tricky part is getting feedback and making sure you're actually improving. It is very common for people to get a piece of advice or feedback, understand it, and then just go right back to trying to hit the ball really hard without knowing if they are doing it right. They just figure their success on whether or not they hit a good shot with that particular swing.

Let's say that one of the things you have to work on is keeping your spine angle constant and keeping your balance in the middle of your feet. A person will say, "Okay, I understand that." And that is that. There is an assumption that understanding it is the same as doing it. They may try it, but generally, they fall right back to how they were swinging before.

Get some information on your swing from someone such as your local pro. Practice with that information in mind until you know whether you are doing it or not. And then do it until it becomes second nature. You have to be able to do it without any thinking, until it is just an automatic part of your swing.

Start at the bottom

There is what you might call a pyramid of fundamentals. The place where you have to start is your connection to the club; how you are holding the club, the way you place your hands on the club. Typically after that, you want to look at your stance, or how your feet are set. This is the way that you stand in preparation to hit a shot.

Putt, putt

Putting is the one thing that you can have the biggest and fastest improvement in because the movements are the least complicated compared with any other part of the game. It is actually easier to become a good putter than it is to become proficient at a full swing.

Now, the average number of putts on the PGA tour is under thirty. Looking at an eighteen-hole round and having each hole be worth two putts, that is actually more than six under par. So if you apply that to someone who is new, along with the fact that a full swing goes through a very large range of motion and moves very fast and there are lots of moving parts, improving is a long-term project and takes an extreme amount of refinement and quite a bit of feel and understanding.

On the putting stroke, there are so many fewer moving parts, and so much less is involved in terms of what is going on physically, that it is much easier, even for a beginner, to approximate the same thing that a PGA Tour member is doing.

Now, obviously pros practice much more and they've been playing a lot longer, so they will have much more control. But it would be a much better bet that someone would achieve thirty putts a round, than that some person would hit twelve greens in regulation.

Grip isn't as important with putting because if you perform a putting stroke correctly, your hands don't move. Watch golf on TV and notice that there are a lot of different grips that seem to work. A putting grip should be comfortable and should allow you to be sensitive to what is happening with the club. Remember to keep the tension out of your grip.

Wedge shots

You can call wedge shots part of the full swing. Those clubs, because they are the shortest with the biggest faces, give you the most amount of loft, so they are the easiest clubs to get a feel for and develop some kind of consistency with. But those are the clubs you want to become deadly accurate with. Those are the clubs that you want to develop the most amount of refinement with because you will be hitting them very frequently and they can save you.

Spend the cash

My take is, if your skill level is high enough, you could almost play with anything. But that also goes for someone who is new. They could almost play with anything and it wouldn't matter because they are on the other side of that curve. The people who really benefit from having equipment that fits them is that huge middle group.

Any player benefits from having clubs that match his physique. Getting a set of clubs that matches your physique and the speed of your swing is more important than getting the latest technological breakthroughs. Get a set of clubs that matches you and don't spend too much money. You don't have to buy the expensive, highly marketed clubs.

20

HOW TO BE A BETTER BOWLER

Chris Barnes, PBA professional

About the Expert: Chris Barnes was the United States Olympic Committee's Athlete of the Year for Bowling in 1994, 1996, and 1997. He was a 2004-05 PBA Player of the Year candidate tying for the Tour lead with five television appearances while capturing his first career major title. He is a winner of the PBA Motel 6 Roll to Riches presented by GEICO, a season-ending special event that awarded him $200,000, the biggest grand prize in PBA history.

Have balls

One of the things that would help most people is to go out and get their own ball. Typically, when you are younger, it is one pound for every year of your age. But one size doesn't fit all when you get older. When they drill bowling balls that you pick off a shelf at a bowling center, most of the time the holes are way too big for the weight you are throwing. Ideally, the thumbhole should just lightly brush the outsides of your thumb.

If you have a weaker wrist or wrist trouble, some kind of wrist support would make sense. If you do get one, make sure it is one that stops motion from breaking your wrist backward. Something that allows movement forward to a cup position is ideal. You don't want your wrist to move backward, because that would render your wrist too weak to really do anything with the ball.

If the shoe fits . . .

Shoes become an advantage when you get to the point where you are recreationally bowling at least once every two weeks. You can buy a nice pair of bowling shoes for $70 to $80. The starter shoes are somewhat helpful, but most of the time there is very little technology in them—just a piece of leather on top of a piece of rubber.

The shoes will give you, on your non-sliding foot, a push-off, or rubber bottom. The sliding shoe will have a better piece of leather and a little bit of a raised heel that you can use for breaking. The cheaper shoes are generally really flat and pretty tacky and actually make it hard to slide.

With footwork, the first thing you need to do is to work on the fundamentals. Make sure your timing is right. In a four-step approach for a right-handed bowler, you want the right foot and the right hand to start at the same time, with the push away. You also want your right step to be approximately the same length as the push away, about twelve to eighteen inches.

As the weight transfers fully to that foot, the ball starts to drop down and by the time the weight goes to your second step, the ball should be between three and eighteen inches past your left ankle. Third step, the ball is at the top of the back swing. And by the fourth step it passes by your ankle.

Use a strategy

There is a strategy in bowling. There is oil applied to the lane, and the oil is typically placed toward the center to provide less friction. As you move to the outside of the lane there is less oil. That allows balls that go a little bit to the outside some friction to hook back.

Going back to the house balls: all the house balls are made out of a super-hard, durable material. They are meant to last for twenty years, and they do. It is kind of like hitting a Pinnacle.

If you want the ball to spin on the green, that is probably not the ball to use.

So ideally, you want a little bit of rotation. The rotation allows you to take advantage of the oil on the lane and achieve the ultimate goal, which is to get some kind of angle of entry into the pocket. The best angle for right-handers is between the one and three pins.

Also, you want a little bit of side rotation with a ball that is at least an entry-level reactive resin ball. You want to play somewhere around the second arrow from the right. That way there is some oil to your left and some friction to your right.

You want to stand on the second dot from the right, and that will allow you some room for the ball to hook from the right and use some of that oil in the middle of the lane.

Straight shooter

For the league bowler who wants to get better, typically, you want to be able to learn how to shoot straight. You want to break your wrist as you pass a rigid point, relaxing the grip pressure and throwing at everything directly with a harder shelled ball, a plastic ball similar to a house ball.

You also want to be more versatile. Understand how to adjust when the ball goes farther left than you want it to. For example, if you have a three, six, ten, you might want to move your feet three boards. If you leave a six, ten, you might want to move your feet two boards.

After that, you'll want to learn how to change speeds. I find that the easiest way to change speeds is to keep your tempo and pace the same, but, if you want to throw it slower, move up twelve to eighteen inches on the approach. The theory there is that you cover less ground in the same amount of time. It is just the opposite to throw it faster.

Another way to improve is to be in shape. My wife is on the national team and we train together. Flexibility, toning, and balance are important.

21

HOW TO WIN (OR AVOID) A FIGHT

Jeff Jarrett, professional wrestler

About the Expert: *Jeff Jarrett is a multiple NWA and WCW World Champion as well as a former WWE Intercontinental Champion. He has held countless wrestling titles and currently serves as executive vice president and a starring perfomer for TNA Wrestling.*

Before getting into a fight, count the guy's friends. If you've got more friends than he does, and you trust your friends, that immediately sets the ground rules. Numbers can overcome anything.

Whether you get into a fight also depends on how mouthy the guy is. You have to size him up. As far as the thought process in a fight, it has to come instinctively. Remember that there are no rules. Go for the eyes. Go for the throat.

If you have to get into a fight, the size of the guy does not matter. The old adage, "The bigger they are, the harder they fall," is true. Size has nothing to do with it. Size matters in some things, but not in a fight.

Remember that there is no such thing as a fair fight. Always play to win.

Avoiding a fight

Pick the right places to go out. Make sure that you know where the security is and where the exits are in case you have to make a quick exit. When you're well known, you have to be prepared to leave quickly in case fights that you have nothing to do with occur. Once you do that, if there is any question, from a legal standpoint, you have to make sure that your security is well in place.

There's no way to teach someone how to avoid or react in a fight. At least, 99 percent of it can't be taught. Your attitude and your instincts are the things that take over in those situations.

In the old days, wrestlers had to win any fights they got into in order to protect their images. That's absolutely not true anymore. There has never been a horse that couldn't be ridden or a cowboy who couldn't be thrown.

There used to be a cowboy named Sputnik Monroe—this is going back to the '60s—and he was a bad-guy wrestler. Now, the carnival was in town through the week and there was going to be wrestling on Saturday night. Well, Sputnik had too many beers to drink and there was a rodeo. The winner of the rodeo was a pretty spunky cowboy who started shooting his mouth off and saying that he could take Sputnik because he was a "phony wrestler."

So Sputnik challenged him, and the little cowboy ended up getting Sputnik and taking it to him pretty good. So the promoter heard about it on Thursday or Friday and did everything in his power to get the cowboy into the ring for a match. The cowboy flat-out refused because he thought it was a setup.

He thought Sputnik had let him win and that he was going to get humiliated in the ring. So the mystique about wrestlers can work positively or negatively.

The best way to avoid a fight would be to let the guy know that it would be in his best interest to avoid it. Take it from a wrestler, the best defense is always a good offense.

Ninety percent of the time, wrestlers—because not only do we get in the ring, but we get a lot of mic time—learn to use our verbal skills. So, you could verbally intimidate or negotiate your way out of a problem.

22

HOW TO GET A JOB

Nick Corcodilos, Asktheheadhunter.com

About the Expert: *Nick Corcodilos is the host of "Ask The Headhunter" and author of* Ask the Headhunter: Reinventing the Interview to Win the Job. *Featured in* The Wall Street Journal, Reader's Digest, USA Today, The New York Times, Fast Company, Working Woman, *and on CNN, CNBC, and MSNBC, Nick's iconoclastic techniques for job search, hiring, and career development are used by job hunters and employers alike. President of North Bridge Group, Inc., Nick Corcodilos has been retained by companies including AT&T, Merrill Lynch, Becton Dickinson, and Procter & Gamble.*

The first step is to be aware of all the myths of job hunting. Don't write a résumé. A résumé is a huge waste of time. People don't get jobs from résumés. A résumé is not a marketing device, and it doesn't sell you. It is a dumb piece of paper that a manager can use to toss you out of the running.

Consider this: You send your résumé to five hundred companies and it sits on a manager's desk while he decides whether he wants to interview you. Meanwhile, my candidate is sitting in the manager's office talking to him about how he's going to help the manager produce profit and contribute to the bottom line.

The difference between a job hunter who uses a résumé and a job hunter who uses and cultivates personal contacts in his industry and in the company he is interested in is simple: One gets the job and one doesn't. Sorry to be so blunt about it, but that is the way the world works.

No résumé?

When you write a résumé, you are working with a ridiculous premise: that going after a lot of companies is a good thing. You might as well go buy a lottery ticket, because it doesn't work that way.

You need to go out and pick a small handful of companies that ring your bells, that excite you, the leaders, the shining lights of the industry that you want to work in. Life is short, so why waste time with anything else?

Use the Internet, go to the library and talk to the reference librarian. Study the company's business. Study its competition. Look at the problems and challenges it is facing, then sit down and ask yourself, "How can I go into this company and help contribute to the bottom line?" If you don't take a profit-based approach, you're wasting your time. You're then just another job candidate; you're just another résumé; you're just another person coming in the door.

Once you've figured out what you can bring to the company's bottom line, put together a little business plan. A business plan basically says, "This is how I would do this job in a way that would be effective and profitable for your business." What you do then is talk with people who work in the company and people who do business with that company.

When you put this business plan together, it indicates that you know about the business, so find out all you can. Talk with vendors, customers, and people who are involved in industry groups that relate to the company. You need to understand what is going on within the organization.

Bingo, now you have something that is better than a résumé. You now have contacts.

People love to talk

People love to talk about their business. As you start to get that insight you learn a lot. That leads you to talk to more people. "Well, gee, who else do you recommend I talk to in the company regarding the marketing department?" This is how you get in the door.

This is how a headhunter helps his own candidate get in the door. It's all about personal contacts, but not about goofy, mercenary networking. It's all about establishing a credible interest in the business and in helping the business. Never ask directly for a job lead—you'll just be referred to the HR department.

Once you get in the door and make these contacts, you can start to make your business plan. Now you can get in to talk to a manager because you've been referred by someone who recognizes that you may be able to bring some value to the operation.

Then what?

You call the manager who has an open position and say, "I've been talking with so-and-so and so-and-so and they've pointed out to me that your operation is growing. I understand that two key problems or challenges that you are facing may be these; correct me if I'm wrong.

"But I've really been trying to study your business and I was wondering if you could give me a little more insight into where your business is going and where you think you might need some help."

If you approach them in an arrogant and presumptuous way, they will blow you off. If you approach them by saying, "So-and-so suggested that I give you a call," that opens up the door. If you feel awkward and don't want to come off as presumptuous, you say, "So-and-so suggested that I give you a call. I have an interest in your business. I don't send out résumés because I'm not out actively looking for a job, but I've got a great interest in your company." Now you have three or four names to drop if you've done your homework right.

When you get there

Let the manager talk a little bit. Ask for a twenty-minute meeting. "Would you have twenty minutes for me to stop by so I can get a little more insight into your operation?" Not many managers get phone calls like that.

If you really want to be bold, you say to the manager, "Look, I know you might think that I'm coming to you from out of left field, and if I seem like a know-it-all, please pardon me, but I've spent quite a bit of time trying to get a sense of how I might be able to contribute something to your operation and I've put together a business plan.

"It's a fifteen-minute presentation. If you've got fifteen minutes for me, I'd like to come by your office. If after five minutes you don't like what I have to say, stop me and I'll leave, no questions asked. I'm not here to waste your time, I'm here because I think I can help you out."

If after that a manager blows you off, it's probably not a place you want to work at, anyway.

Be prepared

You should go up to the white board and write down the answers to what I call the four questions. You need to demonstrate that you understand the work that needs to be done. Question one is, "What problems or challenges is the company facing?"

Question two is, "Can I do the work?" You need to show how you are going to go about doing it.

Question three is, "Can I do the work the way the company wants it done?" In other words, how does it fit into their culture, the way they operate, the way they think? It's got to be a fit.

The final question is, "Can I contribute to the bottom line?" Draw a line on the bottom of the board and write a number, which is your best estimate of what you think you can add to the bottom line as a result of doing the job your way.

Your number can be wildly off, but if you can justify how you came up with it you will impress a smart manager.

That is when you look the manager in the eye and you don't just say, "Thank you for the meeting," you say, "I want to come and work for your team."

The job offer

There are two parts to every job offer. There is the work and there is the compensation. Say to the manager, "We've just established that you want me to work here and I want to work here. Now all that remains is for us to work out the terms." You can make a commitment without getting yourself stuck.

You need to ask yourself three questions before you to negotiate for a job. One, what kind of money would you take to do this job that would make you accept the offer and say, "This is cool, I'll take it." Two, what kind of money would you take that would make you say, "I'll take the job on the spot."

The best thing to do is to leave some money on the table. The third question is how much money would make you jump through the roof with sheer joy. Come up with those three numbers; your objective is to get a number between the second and the third.

If you get a good offer and say, "I bet I can get a little more," you're toast. If you get a good offer, take it. If you want more, justify it on your first review.

Avoid mistakes

Get a hold of those stupid questions that everybody asks, like, "What animal would you be?" and "What is your favorite color?" There are books out there that have them listed, along with the right answers. Bring them with you and if the manager starts in on them, bring them out and say, "You have all the questions, I have all the answers, so let's roll up our sleeves and get to business."

Most people, when looking for a job, don't analyze the job market. Here's the news: Downsizing is up. Seven thousand laid off at a transportation company. A bank cans two thousand. An airline boots four thousand. A communications company drops eighty-five hundred. Jobless claims are on a seesaw ride. The state of the job market makes people worry, and that makes them terrible job hunters.

Headhunters couldn't care less what the job market is doing. Their power stems from their ability to solve a company's problem. They look for employers who need help. When downsizing results in masses of people changing jobs, companies rely on headhunters even more, because it's harder to weed through all those desperate, inappropriate candidates when you're trying to fill a few important positions. In many cases, the same companies that are firing people out one door are hiring people through another and paying fees for help in doing so.

Don't waste time fretting over the news. If headhunters did that, they'd go out of business. Spend your time finding managers who have work that needs to be done. Don't make assumptions about what jobs are or are not available.

People also spend way too much time poring over the want ads. Job hunters look at the online job boards (or the classifieds) and see opportunities beckoning. Headhunters see a big sump, where the troublesome masses collect and spiral away. And that's where headhunters like to see their competition: out of the way, getting processed by personnel jockeys.

When I lived near San Francisco, I had to explain to my frequent east coast guests that the one place they hoped to visit was the one place we would avoid: Fisherman's Wharf. Like the job boards, Fisherman's Wharf is a sump. It's the place San Francisco has set aside to corral loud, unruly, bothersome tourists. It keeps them off the streets. And the city goes to great lengths to convince outsiders that this is the best place to go when you visit.

No self-respecting San Franciscan would waste his or her

time at Fisherman's Wharf. It's a pit. So are the job databases. When five thousand people apply for a job, the job is hardly "available." Simple statistics will tell you that even an outstanding candidate can slip through the cracks while unsophisticated personnel jockeys are screening thousands of applicants. (And that's before they get around to actually interviewing a few hundred.)

Like that little postcard says, "Thank you for submitting your résumé. We are currently evaluating your qualifications. Due to the large number of responses, we will not be able to get back to you any time soon. If ever."

Do you really consider that job available? Go buy a lottery ticket. The other reason these jobs are not really available is because while personnel is reading résumés, some headhunter has met with the hiring manager, submitted three candidates, and is helping one of them evaluate an offer. Personnel doesn't even know this is happening. Beep! Time's up. On to the next résumé database.

23

HOW TO START YOUR OWN BUSINESS

Stephanie Chandler, author, founder,
Businessinfoguide.com

About the Expert: *Stephanie Chandler founded Business-infoguide.com and is the author of* The Business Startup Checklist and Planning Guide: Seize Your Entrepreneurial Dreams! *She is also a freelance writer specializing in business-related articles, a small business advisor for AllExperts.com, a board member for the Northern California Publishers and Authors Association, and a small-business coach.*

There are really three main keys to a successful startup. Those keys are capital, a startup plan, and a marketing strategy.

You need to decide what type of business you want to start. You need to study the industry for your business; study your competition. I am a really big believer in educating yourself on running a business, reading as many books as you can. The Internet is such a great resource for finding information. Join trade associations and read trade magazines.

Of course you have to give your business a name and get a business license. If you are selling merchandise, you have to get a resale license. And a Web site is key for anyone operating a business.

Finding startup cash

There have been some recent studies that show that lack of capital is the main hurdle that prevents people from opening their business. There are a number of ways to find startup capital.

You can try to get a small-business loan. These are easier to get if you are buying an existing business. If you are starting a new business, these loans can be really difficult to get.

Some people like to go after business grants. There is a big misconception out there about them, though. They are not like scholarships, they are not going to take you all the way through, and there aren't enough of them out there. Because of this you have to get really creative in your search for financing.

Friends and family are probably the number-one resource for coming up with money for a business. A lot of people look to home equity lines, which are the same liabilities as a small-business loan. You are personally liable for the money no matter what. And when interest rates are low, a small equity line or second mortgage can be a pretty reasonable way to do it.

I recommend people start small—especially when you don't have a lot of capital. Start small and work your way up. There are a lot of people who dream of opening a restaurant, for example, but that is a very expensive venture to undertake. But you can start small with a little catering business.

If you have big toys, like an extra car or a Jet Ski, and you really want this business, sell those things. Generate some capital any way you can. You can also use credit cards. It makes everyone nervous, but the fact is that this is unsecured debt. You want to be careful. You don't want to get in over your head no matter what you are doing. It is like being a gambler: Never bet more than you can afford to lose. But credit cards are unsecured debt, so you are not going to lose your house.

There is also angel capital. Angel investors are basically looking to invest in business opportunities. A lot of times they are just a regular people. Sometimes they are eccentric, wealthy people who just want to invest in a good business idea. So if you can find angel capital, that is really a great way to get started. There are a couple of Web sites to help you track these people down. First, there is my Web site. For grants you can go to grants.gov. For angel capital there is a site called activecapital.org.

Doing it legally

The licensing is pretty much the same for a service or a retail business. The requirements differ by county, so you have to go to your county offices and see what the requirements are to make sure you are in compliance with local laws. But if you are looking to start something inside a commercial location, you are faced with negotiating a lease, and I highly recommend you get a commercial Realtor to help you with that.

Say you drive by a mall or shopping center and see a FOR LEASE sign and a phone number. It is very easy to pick up the phone and inquire about a space. But if you have never negotiated a lease before, it can be tricky. And you don't pay the Realtor; they're paid by the leaser.

Once that is taken care of you have supply issues. If you are opening a restaurant, for instance, you need restaurant supplies.

Have a plan

Hopefully you have a very solid business plan once you have money and space. You need to deal with the hiring of a staff and plan your marketing strategy. I think a lot of people go wrong by just flipping the light on and expecting people to show up; that is just not how it works.

You need a solid marketing strategy. How are you going to let people know you are there? Marketing means that you need to expose people to your product or service repeatedly. Studies say people need eight exposures to a product before they make a buying decision. So you need to figure out how you are going to get it in front of them over and over and over again without blowing your entire budget.

Advertise

I think the cheapest and best form of advertising you can get is through the media. Any type of media exposure you can get is good. When my bookstore was mentioned in the *Sacramento Bee*, my business doubled. It was a very short article about me and the opening of the store, and people came in droves. So write press releases, send letters to editors and reporters. It is really that simple.

Whether you should pay to advertise depends on the type of business you run. Restaurants have a really good return rate on advertising because they can offer coupons and because people like to try new restaurants. You can try direct mail. You can advertise in coupon books like Valpak. There are pennysavers, TV, and radio. It all depends on your budget and your target demographic. You also want to look at where your competition is advertising.

When have you failed?

You really have to look at your overall business plan to know if you have failed. If you want out of a business you can sell it. But it is near impossible to sell a business that isn't profitable. You could try to bring in another investor rather than just give up.

I have watched a couple of businesses close recently. They just ran out of money. It's unfortunate, but you can avoid that by having a sound business plan. A lot of people don't like to write business plans, and some even say that they don't need one, but you really use it if you are taking it to the bank to get a loan, and it is such an important tool in understanding your business because it forces you to think about every aspect of your business. It will help you with your financials, and how you are going to turn a profit. So hopefully you'll work on it and study your market and set yourself up for success.

Make a new plan, Stan

You can always hire someone to write it for you, but I recommend that you do that only if you are going to take it to the bank. There are numerous books on the topic, and even some software. There is a free business-plan outline on my Web site.

What's next?

How to take things to the next level depends on your vision. You could open another location. You could franchise your business and open franchise opportunities. And then again, some people like to remain small.

I've been in Silicon Valley for eleven years, and when I left corporate America, many people said to me, "I wish I had the courage to do what you did." I think that people are held back by fear when it comes to starting a business. You can minimize that fear by being prepared. Get everything together, and get your ducks in a row.

24

HOW TO TACKLE HOME IMPROVEMENTS

Kevin O'Connor, host, *This Old House*

About the Expert: *Nominated for an Outstanding Service Show Host Emmy in his debut season, Kevin O'Connor is the host of* This Old House. *He also serves as on-air talent for* Ask This Old House *and* Inside This Old House. *O'Connor also serves on the editorial board of* This Old House *magazine, published by This Old House Ventures, Inc.*

Most people can do a lot more than they think they can. Be confident that you can do it. The work is a combination of a lot of really simple tasks. It's about building them up on top of one another and using the right ones in the right places. Sawing wood and drilling holes and weighing out designs and things like that are all really basic tasks most people can do. In the end, it's about putting them all together.

You can do it

Something I did that probably would have scared off a lot of people is retiling the bathroom. It's a combination of relatively simple tasks: of making sure that your subfloor is straight, that your subfloor is strong, that you put on a backboard that goes down correctly, that those joints are sealed, that you have a proper mastic on top of that, that the tile is laid correctly, that the drying time and the consistency of the mastic are appropriate, and that the grout is the right kind and applied properly and cleaned up at the right time. This might seem like a daunting task, and it's something that a lot of people want to farm out to a professional, but each of those individual steps is very basic.

What steps to take

Some of the steps you learn growing up, some of them you read in a book, some of them you get from our and other television shows, and some you learn from the Web. There has definitely been a proliferation of easily available home-improvement information.

It's just a massive industry and there are tons of resources. Today, in an hour, you can find twenty different sources on how to put down an inset for tile. Most will be accurate and, in the end, the task itself is pretty easy.

Information is out there, and like I said, the individual steps are fairly straightforward. You need to understand the order and how you combine them. You can't fool yourself into thinking that the first time you do it or even the third time you do it, it'll be at the level of skill a professional would do, but you can do it.

When to go pro

In some cases you need to use a professional. It's absolutely important for most electrical work, and for a lot of plumbing, too.

There can also be permit issues. In Massachusetts, for example, you're not allowed to do either of those two tasks yourself. You have to get a license. However, the majority of states allow you to do some level of plumbing and electrical work. Check the regulations for your state. Generally those regulations are there for pretty good reasons.

In addition to electrical and plumbing, there is the structural stuff. For example, we are renovating the kitchen downstairs and we took out a wall and created a sixteen-foot stand. We eventually just threw in the towel and I got an engineer. Why do you mess around with structural issues? Don't. Just find someone.

Pros may not help you

I wish I could say it was easy, but it's tough to get a pro to oversee or certify your work. I'm fortunate that I actually can, just because of my job. On a job I did recently, my electrician was more than happy that I hung the electrical boxes, and it gave me the flexibility of being able to put them where I wanted, doing it at my pace. But not a lot of guys want to supervise. They want come in and do it.

How do you pick a contractor?

There are a lot of benefits that come to me as the host of *This Old House*, and even I have problems. This is a really hard question to answer. You have to dig deep, you have to get recommendations, you have to actually follow up on them, and you have to be skeptical of them. You have to really ask the tough questions and ask for three recommendations.

Get a sense of the guy when he shows up. Does he know what he's talking about, does it seem to make sense, is he timely, does he have a truck with everything he needs? I hate to say it but I had a contractor who was such a good faker that he fooled me. But when he showed up the first day he was borrowing my hammer and my extension cord. A framer who doesn't have a freaking hammer just raises a red flag.

No matter what you do, it won't always be enough. Go on reputation. Don't be afraid to spend a little more. Going for a low cost will usually get you low-cost work.

I can tell you personally I've used the big box store referral services with great success. I think what's good about it is that they are using local tradesmen who have been in the business for a long time. It's not like the guy who's walking it down showing you where the items are is installing your siding. They're using siding contractors.

What about quality?

You should be concerned about the quality when you go anywhere, but I'm actually a fan of the box stores.

When I was a kid, I loved walking into my local hardware

store with my dad and there were these three guys who worked there my entire life, probably long before I was born. Those stores were great, but you know what? They had a fraction of the stuff you needed, and they weren't open on the weekends. And when I walked through the back gate to the lumberyard no one paid attention to me. I wasn't a contractor. I wasn't buying a flatbed worth of materials.

It was intimidating, and for better or for worse, these big box stores cater to homeowners doing the weekend job and when I walk through that lumberyard gate, I'm as important as Tom Silva.

If you could only fix one thing . . .

I would have to say the kitchen. The Realtor associations and home-builder associations would generally agree that the kitchen is most important to the resale value of a home, but I think it is also the most satisfying to the homeowners as well. We spend more and more of our time in the kitchen.

Avoid these mistakes

Don't take the short view. I make this mistake frequently. A lot of this stuff is time consuming and difficult. It's not impossible, but it is a challenge. Because many people aren't proficient, home improvement can be complicated. As a result, it's easy to want to get things done as quickly as possible.

It goes for every project you do, especially if you can't afford something. If you just don't have the funds right now, honestly, wait a year. And don't cheap out on materials. Fight hard to be able to do it right because the satisfaction will be greater in both the short and long terms.

25

HOW TO BUY A CAR

Jeff Ostruff, consumer advocate, CarBuyingTips.com

About the Expert: *Jeff Ostroff has been running Car BuyingTips.com since 1997 and has appeared on numerous television and radio programs. He is also the creator of Bridaltips.com and has helped thousands of people avoid getting scammed.*

Before you go to the car dealer there is work you have to do. You have to know what your credit score is. Because that is the single biggest mistake that car buyers make—not knowing what their finances will be able to support.

Virtually everybody has some issue with their credit score, something that's wrong with their credit report. You can check your report instantly online, and then see what is keeping your score down—especially if something is being reported incorrectly.

You should also make sure that your credit card balances are below 50 percent. As soon as they get over 50 percent, that is when your credit score begins to really drop rapidly, and many lenders may refuse to lend you money. For example, if you have a $2,000 credit limit, you want to keep it below $1,000 in outstanding debt. If you have any old accounts you don't use anymore, dump 'em. Close them, because they are just sitting there. They are just excess baggage that's dragging down your score.

Know everything first

We tell people to get the pricing research done ahead of time. One Web site to try is fightingchance.com. You should know how much your car should cost to within a couple hundred dollars before you even pull into the parking lot. This includes pricing out all the options.

We tell people to print out all that stuff, get a hold of their credit report, and get pre-approved for a car loan as well, all online. There are a number of sites, like E-Loan and Capital One, that are useful. For example, I just bought a new Lexus SUV last year; on Tuesday afternoon at two o'clock I applied at Capital One and a half an hour later I got an e-mail that I was approved. Because they are in California and I'm in Florida, they were able to FedEx the check the same day, and I had the check the next morning at ten A.M. So not even twenty-four hours after I applied the check was in my hand.

Getting yourself pre-approved online is the best way to go, because that way if the dealer doesn't give you financing that is better than or equal to that, you just give them the check from the online financer.

Make sure the dealership sees you with what I call "the folder" full of research. Once they see that, they'll know that you've done your research and your homework and that they probably won't be able to pull half their sales tricks on you.

What to watch for

Many of the tricks take place in the finance office. For example, "The bank requires you to buy this warranty, otherwise you won't get a loan." Though dealers quite commonly say this, it is pretty much illegal to tell somebody. It is a violation of the Fair Credit Act.

Another common one is "You have to buy this VIN number etching on the glass, otherwise the bank won't approve the loan." And they usually charge $400, but you can buy the kit that etches the number onto the glass online for much less.

Tricks are pulled everywhere. Never think, A major dealership would never do that. If there's a commission, there'll be a trick. There are bad seeds everywhere. You can't make assumptions.

So as long as you're on the lookout, you can thwart it. We like to empower consumers and send them to the dealers with a lot of knowledge so that none of the scams can be pulled on them.

Don't haggle

We don't think you should haggle over options. We have an offer spreadsheet to help you calculate your offer to the dealer. It's based on the whole car. You don't want to nitpick over every little option. If you've come up with a price, then you can negotiate with that.

You can look up if there are factory-to-dealer incentives in addition to rebates on sites like ours. (There are actually two different types of rebates—to the customer and to the dealer.)

Quite often you'll look and see there's anywhere from $500 to $1,500 factory-to-dealer cash. Many dealers are willing to give that up in order to move the car. So the dealer's true cost is really invoice price minus holdback, minus rebates. Many people have taken our spreadsheet, printed it out, faxed it to the dealer, and gotten them to come right down to that price with very little effort.

Mistakes you can make

While you're in there and negotiating, you don't want to end up a monthly payment buyer. A lot of dealers love to quote monthly payments. If you look at all the dealership ads, they all promote monthly payments. That's because by doing that, they're shielding from you the APR you're paying. They are shielding from you the real price of the car, and they are shielding from you the bogus options they throw in at the end.

What they do is find a monthly payment that you're happy with. That's why they always ask, "What monthly payment were you looking for?" And so whatever you tell them, say $300 a month, they'll stretch that out over however many months it takes to make the total amount equal $300 a month.

They can even come in at $275, but all they did was stretch the same amount of money over seventy-two months. You're paying more over the long haul. People fall for that sleight of hand all the time. The best way to negotiate the purchase is by the actual selling price of the car, not by the monthly payments.

Do you need a warranty?

A lot of people e-mail me and say, "The guy swore to God that he didn't put a warranty in there. But when I got home and read the papers, there it was." And I always have to tell these people, "Why the hell didn't you see it when you were reading it in there, before you signed it?" They spend more time analyzing a watermelon in the grocery store than they do the closing papers for a $20,000 car.

Getting a warranty or not is really about your comfort level. It's almost like buying insurance: You hope you never need it. Some of the better warranties provide you with towing and rental car reimbursement.

It really boils down to how long you plan to keep the car. If you're going to keep it beyond the manufacturer's warranty, then you might want to consider it, because when the warranty expires, that is when all hell's going to break lose.

Buy or lease

Leasing is great, but only for a very small portion of the population—much smaller than most people, or car dealers, even think. The main reason is that a lease is a three-year contract. It's like joining a gym. Have you ever heard of anyone who signed up for a gym and then tried to get out of that contract? The gym will take you to court, and it's the same with a leasing company.

When you lease—say you lease a car for three years—you're only paying for 50 percent of the car. That's why your payments are less—because you're only paying 50 percent of that depreciation over the three years. But if you lease, that means that you're going to be making those monthly payments for as long as you have the car. Whereas if you buy a car, theoretically, you could have it paid off in three years, and then drive it for longer.

Leasing also has fees associated with it that a car loan doesn't. When you sign the lease papers, there is usually a $500 dealer acquisition fee. Then, when you drop off the car at the end of the lease, there is a lease disposition fee that most people don't know about because it is buried in the fine print. That is usually $300–$400. So now you're up to $1,000 just in wasted fees that do nothing for you.

And if you go over mileage you can expect to pay. The people I hear from mostly come in at between $2,000 and $5,000 in penalties, which is something that people don't think about before they sign a lease.

You also have to have four matching tires on your car when you turn it in. If you don't the leasing company will charge you the full retail price for four new tires.

Most leases won't allow you to move out of state, another "gotcha" that catches a lot of people. You have to project out three years, and there are too many unknowns in life for most people for a solid lease contract.

Other tips

Don't trade in a car that you owe money on. We get a lot of complaints from people who trade in a car they owe money on and the dealer doesn't pay it off. The problem is that that there's usually nothing in writing. Then people get angry calls from their banks three months later. And you can't use the excuse, "The dealer was supposed to . . ." because the bank doesn't care. Your name was on the contract. Make the dealer put it in writing, and then you're covered.

But still, all you are doing by trading in a car that you owe money on is transferring the debt. The payments may be lower because the dealer stretches it out over six or seven years, but you don't want to pay for the same car for seven years. We tell people four years is the longest you should finance a loan. If you can't pay for it in four years, you shouldn't be buying it.

The last tip is that the end of the month is usually a good time to buy. Model changeover time, between August and November, is also a really good time. Manufacturers will drop in all sorts of incentives during that time just to get the old inventory out.

26

HOW TO DECLARE BANKRUPTCY

Audrey Blondin, former Connecticut Director of the
National Association of Consumer Bankruptcy Attorneys

About the Expert: *Audrey Blondin is an attorney who has practiced law in Torrington, Connecticut, for twenty-five years in the areas of real estate, bankruptcy, wills, and probate, and she served as the Connecticut Director of the National Association of Consumer Bankruptcy Attorneys from 2002 to 2005.*

The first step in filing for bankruptcy is picking an attorney. The important thing to remember is that if you are in a financial crisis situation, the only person who can really provide the service you need is an attorney. As with any attorney, the best way to pick one is by reference—by talking with and getting a reference from someone who has had the same problems you are having or who knows of someone by reputation. That is the best way to find any professional.

Pick right

When getting an attorney, look at their years of experience. Obviously the more years someone has been practicing in that particular field, the more experience they have, and the more it is likely that they have seen situations like yours and they know how to handle them.

The other thing to look for is credentials. Are they a member of the local and state bar associations? Are they a member of a particular part of the bar association? Are they a member of a national bankruptcy association like the American Bankruptcy Institute or the National Association of Consumer Bankruptcy Attorneys?

Don't be "preparered"

There are many different types of organizations and individuals out there that bill themselves as bankruptcy petition preparers. They are not attorneys, they are not licensed to practice law, and legally they cannot represent you at a bankruptcy hearing.

They are proliferating because there is a provision in the bankruptcy code that allows for a petition preparer, but as is often the case, an inch is taken as a mile and they are really becoming a force. It is not in the client's best interest to be represented in this type of a situation without an attorney because the impact can last years. When you file for bankruptcy, it stays on your credit report for anywhere from seven to ten years, and if it's not done right it can follow you throughout your whole life.

Why file?

The three main reasons people file for bankruptcy are divorce, loss of job, and uninsured medical debt.

There are forty-four million Americans right now who do not have any medical insurance, so there is much potential for this type of bankruptcy. To put the issue of uninsured medical debt into perspective, in the two years before filing for bankruptcy, 22 percent of families went without food, 30 percent had a utility shut off, 61 percent went without needed medical care, and half failed to fill a doctor's prescription. So to put it bluntly, get whatever coverage you can.

How do I know?

The process of going through a bankruptcy usually takes a few months. First you must decide if this is the right move for you.

The first thing you should look at is whether your debts far exceed your assets. If you have a house worth $300,000 and you owe $100,000 on the mortgage and you have $50,000 in credit debt, you should not be thinking of filing for bankruptcy. There are some states where those assets, like the equity in your home, are exempt. They give you an unlimited homestead exemption. You can file for bankruptcy in Florida even if you have a million-dollar house that you own free and clear.

Typically, if you have under $40,000 in equity in your house, you can file. In other words, if the difference between what your house is worth and what you own is under $40,000 you might consider filing Chapter 7 bankruptcy.

You should also have a job. That isn't a requirement, but there is a presumption that when you take this debt under the bankruptcy code, you have the ability to repay it. So you should have a job, your debts should far outweigh you assets, and there should be no other way to get yourself out of debt.

Time to file

Once you know you should file, you should consult your bankruptcy attorney. Bring all your bills and documentation of your assets and the attorney will review all the material and put it together into what we call a petition. Right now, there is an informal means test, so you still must qualify.

Your attorney should be able to direct you to the type of bankruptcy that would best suit you. Do you qualify for the fresh start with Chapter 7, or should you go first to Chapter 13?

Once the determination is made, the documents are prepared. You should also have two years of income-tax returns and six months of pay stubs on hand. From there your attorney can more easily guide you through the rest of the process, which more or less provides financial information for review. Once your Chapter 7 bankruptcy is approved, your debts are eliminated.

Chapter 7

There are two main types of bankruptcy: Chapter 7 and Chapter 13. Chapter 7 bankruptcy is a procedure in which you file what is called a bankruptcy petition in federal court, to the U.S. Trustee's office. There are different districts in which you can file, so where you live will dictate where you file.

When you file this group of papers, what you are doing is asking for a discharge of your debt. In the past, you didn't really have to have a reason or show any income limit to file Chapter 7 bankruptcy. Pretty much anyone who filed was granted a Chapter 7 bankruptcy.

Previously there wasn't a means test, so you could have been making $100,000 and still filed for Chapter 7 bankruptcy. That is no longer the case. For the last seven years, so-called bankruptcy proposals for bankruptcy reform have been introduced to Congress. Senate Bill 256, which covers this issue, became effective on October 17, 2005.

It has become more difficult for people who need a fresh start to file Chapter 7 bankruptcy because it creates a strict means test. In other words, the IRS would say that a particularly sized family should spend X amount a week on food, and Y amount a week on rent, and if you don't fall within those guidelines they are likely to deny you.

Payback time

The trend is to push people from filing a Chapter 7, which is a discharge of your debts that can be filed once every six years, to a Chapter 13. A Chapter 13 is a repayment plan.

It is a way of taking all of your debt and, according to these guidelines, paying a percentage of that debt based on your income and what you have left over, or the amount of money you're "supposed" to have left over at the end of every month. You make these payments between a three- or five-year period, and at the end you have been given your fresh start.

The problem is that most Chapter 13 bankruptcies end up converting to Chapter 7 because the reason you got in this mess in the first place is that you lost your job, don't have health insurance, got a divorce, or are in a life-threatening situation, and the chances of you pulling it all together are really remote.

Avoid the mistakes

One important way to avoid bankruptcy is to not use credit cards as a means for paying for everything. When cards come in the mail, destroy them. That is the key.

Credit card companies continually send out billions of dollars in unsolicited, pre-approved credit card applications. They send them to people who are no longer alive, and to dogs, cats, and college students. College students are one huge group that is being preyed upon by these companies. "Fill it out and get a free T-shirt," many companies entice. A lot of these kids don't have jobs, but now have a $2,500 credit limit that gets the ball rolling toward debt.

You also want to avoid paying credit card debt over a long period of time. Ask your credit card company how long it will take to pay off your debt while making the minimum payment. "If you borrow X amount, it will take you twenty-five years at the Y minimum payment to do that."

You also want to look at your interest rates. There are what are called "teaser rates," where, for example, you start out at 10 percent, but after six months, it jumps up to 28 percent. The credit card companies also have the right, without your knowledge, to run your credit score. And if they see something they don't like, they can hike up your interest rate without your even knowing.

Choose your friends carefully

A lot of people who find themselves in credit card trouble go to a credit-counseling company. More often than not, that is a bad idea. You see the commercials all the time on TV. Often I have bankruptcy clients who have gone to these places because they are desperate and will try anything to avoid bankruptcy. Unfortunately, with the 2005 law, credit counseling is now mandatory prior to filing and prior to granting your discharge. This is an added expense of $200 to $500.

There is a fallacy that people file bankruptcy because they just don't care, or are deadbeats, and that is just wrong. People file for bankruptcy as a last resort. If they go to a credit-counseling firm, they go with the idea that they will pay a monthly payment and eventually work off their debt.

But I have had clients who repeatedly paid thousands of dollars to these agencies, sometimes for years, and the debt has never gone down. The reason is that all you are doing by going to one of these agencies is transferring your debt. They buy up all your debt, and now you are paying them instead of someone else.

27

HOW TO BUY A HOUSE

Bill Janovitz, Realtor, musician

About the Expert: *Bill Janovitz is the lead singer of Buffalo Tom and an accomplished songwriter. He is also a real estate agent for Coldwell Banker in Lexington, Massachusetts.*

Before you start looking for a house, at least in this bull real estate market, a pre-approval for a mortgage is an essential component of the process. You have to make sure your finances are in order and you have to have a letter of pre-approval that accompanies the offer. Here in Massachusetts, no offer is good without a $1,000 dollar bonded check and a pre-approval.

Pre-approval means that they have checked out at least a credit report. A pre-approval is based on a verification of the financial information, while pre-qualification is just based on what you told the lender.

Where to look

Some people seem to have a good idea of where they want to live. My personal decisions are based on proximity to Boston, but for most people it's primarily about school systems. If you buy in a town that has a good school system, real estate will increase in value much more than in a town with a bad one.

The one tip I give people is that I really do recommend buying the most house you can possibly afford at that time.

What does a Realtor do?

Real estate agents tend to come in later in the transaction these days because most people are really savvy about the Internet. They can do a lot of the grunt work on their own (which is fine with me as long as they eventually give me a call).

You certainly can't learn everything on the Internet, and yet I do find people who are reluctant to make the leap to a real estate agent. When they eventually do, they're more satisfied. I spend forty hours a week doing this, and two or three days a week I'm just previewing houses. I get an idea of what different people want and I can narrow the search down because the Internet offers far too many possibilities for someone to check out on their own.

One agent

If you're buying a house it's important to get an agent you are comfortable with. Stick to them and make sure they're working for you. Remember that you don't necessarily have to be paying them. They are usually paid out of the eventual transaction.

I do not recommend working with more than one agent. If you're not happy and you're moving for a reason, fine, but to bop around from agent to agent is doing yourself a disservice. Each time you'll have to go through the process of familiarizing an agent with what you're looking for.

In certain states it's important to know what the law is and who's representing whom. I think that's a really important aspect of the process.

Make me an offer

As a buyer's agent, I show my clients what has sold in that area and in what price range. I let them know what the mortgage market has been like in the last month or so and I'll let them know if they should make an offer. Sometimes houses sell over the asking price, and sometimes they sell under.

When you make an offer you usually have to bring a deposit check. Every state is different. The components of the offer are generally contingent upon securing financing. Another major contingency is the inspection, which I recommend no matter what.

What's next?

At that point you usually get a draft of the sale agreement. Get a lawyer involved as soon as possible. Some people try to bypass the lawyer stage. You can never be too safe. I get a lawyer to look at the person's draft as soon as possible. One way to save on the attorney's fee is to find out who the bank attorney is going to be, and they'll usually do the sale for you for a reduced fee.

The closing

In the offer stage you're spelling out when you propose to close, when you'll have the inspection done, and other details. Dates are as important as the price for a lot of people.

If anything comes up in the inspection that you want addressed by the seller, you usually have that spelled out as an addendum in the sale offer. I always recommend that you get the work done yourself and ask for a price cut because otherwise it will end up getting done cheaply by the seller.

Once you have a sale agreement, then the bank will order an appraisal. If all that comes out okay, you then have a closing. If the closing goes well, you leave it owning the house.

28

HOW TO TRAVEL CHEAPLY

Sheryl Mexic, owner, Biddingfortravel.com

About the Expert: *Sheryl Mexic is the owner and operator of Biddingfortravel.com and a renowned expert on how to use Priceline.com.*

The first thing to know is that there is no single place that's going to have the best deal all the time. That's a very common question—"Where is the best place to get the best deal?"

So, where do you start? I prefer to start with hotel Web sites. Find out which hotels are in the area you are visiting. All of the hotels, at least the major brands, have best-rate guarantees on their Web sites. I go there and jot down the best rate for my stay, and then I search as many Web sites as I can.

How many you search depends on what value you place on your time. Are you willing to spend an hour to search Orbitz, Travelocity, Travelweb—all of the travel Web sites out there? There is a chance that you are going to find a deal that is a lot better on one of these sites, but there is no way to know.

The best-rate guarantee works a little differently on each hotel company's site. With Hilton, for example, if you find a rate of $100 a night on their site and go to Expedia and find $95, Hilton will honor the lower rate and, following your stay, will send you a $50 dollar American Express gift check. Another Web site gives you one night free. I know of a couple of sites that give you the first night free, and if it's a one-night stay, your entire stay is free. I believe Marriott will match the better rate and then give you 25 percent off that. Each one works a little differently.

However, the hotels have gotten greedy as this best-rate

guarantee has progressed over the last couple of years. Star-wood and Intercontinental Hotel Group were the ones that started this a couple of years ago. They now require that the room description on the rate display be exactly the same on the competing Web site as on their site to honor the guarantee. The guarantees are being honored less frequently than before, but I do still read reports of people being able to enforce them and being compensated as promised.

Fly, fly away

Booking the cheapest airfare works the same way as with the hotels. You have to check as many sources as possible. You would think you'd get the best fare from the airline's own Web site, but that's not always true. I would say it's true more than 90 percent of the time, but you have to check every airline that flies the route you're going, as well as every major travel agency Web site.

If your travel period is a very popular travel period, I wouldn't wait to book your fare. Say, for example, that you are traveling to Florida in March; the chances of a rate or a fare going down for March travel is not good because March is the busiest month of the year.

Then, there are last-minute deals. There is no best time to book. Sometimes you will get the best deal if you book in advance and sometimes it will be better if you wait until the last minute. If you are flexible and your trip is dependent upon whether you get a good deal, then you have nothing to lose by waiting. If this is a confirmed trip that you are going to take, there is no way to know when the best time to book is.

Also, Travelzoo is a site you can subscribe to and get a weekly e-mail with all of their deals. You don't actually book on their site—they just advertise exceptional deals.

When to bid

Priceline bidding is my expertise. The bottom line is that if you are flexible and you don't have to stay at a particular hotel—you just want to take advantage of a particular area— then Priceline is the way to go. Over 90 percent of the time, Priceline will offer the best deal, bar none.

That does not necessarily go for the package deals on Priceline, for a couple of reasons. With the package deals you have to buy airfare. For the last couple of years Priceline has not offered a viable option for airfare bidding in most cases. Using them for airfare has gotten to be a good deal in most cases only when you're up against a very high fare at the last minute.

There are some routes out there that are always expensive. Say you're going from Boise to Charlotte and that route never gets below $450. That's a good time to use Priceline; maybe you could expect to pay around $300.

Priceline's airline ticket product requires that you have a lot of flexibility. You have to be willing to leave at six in the morning or arrive at your destination at midnight. For a lot of people, that may not be an option.

Drawbacks

I have not had any problems with the hotels Priceline has put me in, but I've heard of some. I've read thousands of reports on Priceline and I have heard of some hotels giving Priceline customers inferior treatment. I've never experienced it, but I don't doubt that it happens.

The other problem can be the rating of the hotels. This is a problem on all travel sites, and Priceline, certainly, is not immune to it. Priceline did a study about a year ago that showed that Hotwire (another travel site) actually sells hotel rooms at a higher price than Priceline over 50 percent of the time. Remember that just because a hotel from one brand is rated one way in one market, it won't necessarily be the same someplace else. There are three-star Marriott hotels and four-star Marriott hotels.

Bid tips

Of course, I recommend visiting Biddingfortravel.com and reading our FAQs. We give you the basis for how to put together your bid. I find that people, before they come to my site, make mistakes in both directions. They come in too low or too high.

As far as hotel bidding goes, it depends on the area for which you're bidding. For example, I just bid on a hotel near Dulles Airport in Washington for a friend of mine, and it took $100 for a three-star hotel room. In another airport zone you might be able to get a three-star hotel room for $30–$35 dollars. There's no consistency. That's why seeing on my site what other people have paid really helps.

I really stress that you can't base your bidding strategy solely on the rates other people have paid. You also have to do your research. Some hotels can have very low rates one night and be sold out the next.

Everyone should remember that bidding for travel is not for everyone. If you have specific needs that you have to have met, you should use a travel agent.

One more tip that I have—and this applies to any type of travel—is that when you find a rate that is really, really good and your plans are firm, book it. An hour later it may not be there. If you know that you're looking at a great deal, don't try to get it down another ten or twenty dollars.

29

HOW TO GET OUT OF DEBT

Debby Fowles, author, *The Everything Personal Finance in Your 20s and 30s Book*

About the Expert: *Debby Fowles is the author of* The Everything Personal Finance in Your 20s & 30s Book *and* 1000 Best Smart Money Secrets for Students. *She has extensive business experience, including fourteen years as controller and ten years on the board of directors of a rapidly growing biomedical research company near Washington, D.C.*

A lot of people assume that all debt is credit card debt, but a lot of people get in over their heads by buying either too much house or too much car, and what happens is they really can't afford the house or the car that they bought, and those payments are more than they can afford, and they start to use credit cards to get other things.

There are plenty of people who overuse credit cards and get into trouble with them alone, but sometimes you have to look deeper to really find the true culprit. It's not always as obvious as just credit cards.

It starts early

Debt starts with younger and younger people these days. Young adults are not really taught how to manage their money, and they tend to get into trouble when they go to college. Once they get out of school they think they're going to be making good money so that they will be able to pay off the debt, but it doesn't really work that way for most people.

The obvious answer is to avoid using credit cards as an extension of your income. We need to teach this to young people. There's no widely accepted curriculum in school that includes this life lesson. There are no requirements in most states for personal finance courses.

Get your report

Once you decide it's time to get out of debt, get a copy of your credit report and score to see how credit lenders are looking at you.

Keep in mind, too, that the majority of reports have mistakes in them. Since everything in there affects your rates on insurance, whether you can rent an apartment, and even interest rates on your credit cards, you really should make sure everything in there is accurate. Go to the three credit reporting bureaus (Experian, Equifax, and TransUnion), all online, and get one from each, or go to myfico.com.

Digging out

The process of getting out of debt is actually very simple. It's the execution of the process that some people have trouble with.

You have to have the desire to do it and the discipline for the long term. First, know how much debt you have. Many people have as many as ten or twelve credit cards and they don't ever sit down and say, "What does it all add up to?"

Until you really know that number and what you're dealing with, I don't think you can effectively work on paying it off. You have to face that unpleasant reality. Sit down and make a list of every credit card, balance, interest rate, and minimum payment. The "snowball" is a popular term for a very common method of paying off credit card debt, and I propose the same thing to people, except I call it "the credit crunch."

Once you've made your list, start off by paying the minimum payment on every credit card except the one with the highest interest rate. On that one pay everything you can. That reduces your overall interest cost because obviously you're paying more on the one with the highest rate. When that first credit card is paid off, then you start paying as much as you can on the one with the next highest rate while paying the minimum on all the others, and so on.

Consolidate or separate?

A true consolidation loan is frequently not a good deal because it's often at a higher interest rate than that of the original debt. Some of the "we roll all your debts into one payment" services are legitimate, but you have to be careful. I would recommend using one of the agencies of the NFCC (National Foundation for Credit Counseling), and even then you have to be careful because in the last couple of years a few of those agencies have not been as up-front as they should have been.

Watch the traps

Watch out for the large up-front fee. Reputable firms will usually sit down with you and give you free counseling to develop a budget and come up with a plan. They'll negotiate with the credit card company for you, try to get a lower interest rate or a short moratorium on your payments until you can get things under control.

They will then set up a plan for you in which you pay them a set amount every month and they disburse that payment to the various creditors. This is a good idea if you can't create a budget yourself.

Calling your credit card company and asking for a lower rate actually works pretty well in some instances. The key is to do it before you've gotten into trouble with late payments and have lowered your credit.

Making payments on time is very important. A late payment can have a quick impact on your whole credit situation. You could make a late payment on one account and it might affect, for instance, your car insurance.

No way out

For most people there is a way out, but there are definitely times when bankruptcy is the only option.

If you're in trouble because of credit card debt, you should do everything possible to pay off your obligations. I believe bankruptcy is more for people who have gotten into debt over their head because of such things as the loss of a job, medical bills, or divorce. But the common wisdom says if you owe more in credit card debt than your annual salary, you might be a good candidate for bankruptcy.

Avoid making the same mistakes

The biggest mistake people make while paying off their debt is to continue to use the credit card. A lot of people do that even though they're trying to pay down their other debt. However, I still recommend keeping a credit card. If you close the account, it affects your credit score because part of your credit score is based on how much of your available credit you actually use.

You always want to have one card that has some credit available so that if you really do get in a pinch, you can use it.

No easy answers

There are really no easy ways to get out of debt. It takes time and discipline to get everything paid off. If you have no late payments for about three years, you usually can get credit without any problem.

30

HOW TO GET A TABLE AT A POPULAR RESTAURANT

Jonathan Waxman, chef/owner, New York's Barbuto
As told to Douglas Trattner

About the Expert: *The chef and owner of Barbuto, Jonathan Waxman was the chef at Michael's Restaurant in Santa Monica, California, and introduced California cuisine to New York with the opening of the wildly successful Jams restaurant in 1984. He opened Washington Park in 2002, which received two stars from* The New York Times. *Barbuto, Waxman's latest, opened last year in the West Village.*

At Barbuto, which is an Italian restaurant where the menu changes every day, I set aside a percentage of the tables for walk-ins. I've been doing this for a few years now, so I kind of know the drill. Invariably, we have customers who say they are my best friend, regardless if I've ever seen them, met them, or otherwise. "I'm a friend of Jonathan's and I want a table right now," they say. We also have a local crowd, and the last thing you want to do is piss off the local crowd. They are very loyal, so we always hold back tables. Invariably, we always find tables for people who want them.

Tables also open up because there are always no-shows on busy nights. People always change the size of their parties. People never come on time. These are the three factors that keep you on your toes. At Jams we would have close to 40 percent no-shows on a Saturday night. These days, that rate is down to 15 percent or less.

girl's not going to be too impressed. Also, if he orders a beer, he isn't going to look very sophisticated.

A glass of red wine is a pretty safe and masculine way to go. You can also order a martini, as long as it's vodka or gin—but no specialty martinis. Don't ever ask for the martini list. Let the girl do that. (The only exception comes either with dessert or instead of dessert, where an espresso martini is perfectly acceptable.)

Any guy on a first date, or any other date for that matter, should remember that the only time it's okay for a guy to order a Cosmopolitan is when he is by himself, or maybe with his mother.

Martinis and the classics

The martini has been bastardized by many different ingredients. Nowadays, you can take any drink out there, put it in a martini shaker, strain it, and put it in a martini glass, and all of a sudden it's supposed to be a martini.

I am a fan, however, of all of the classic cocktails, which are making a bit of a comeback. Sidecars, Stingers, Manhattans, and Old Fashioneds have all had a bit of a resurgence. But those cocktails, which are based on darker liquors such as scotch and bourbon, came back into fashion when cigars became popular again. Even though both fads seem to be dying down, it's always appropriate to order one of these classic drinks.

Call your liquor

Some people always call their brand regardless of what cocktail they happen to be drinking. Women order Grey Goose cosmopolitans because they think that Grey Goose is the chi-chi vodka.

But if you're ordering anything that has juice in it, you're wasting your money because you can't taste the difference any-

Big or small?

If you're looking to walk in, the size of your party really doesn't matter in getting a table. Sometimes deuces (two-seat tables) are harder to get than a four- or six-top. There is no true rule here.

The quieter nights in the restaurant business are Sunday, Monday, and Tuesday, and those are definitely the best nights to try to just walk up and be seated. As for times, we give everyone the same drill: Try 6:30 or 10 P.M. Everyone calls and asks for eight o'clock. I start laughing and say, "You really are kidding me, right? You're calling me on Friday night for a Saturday night reservation for eight P.M., and you're doing this in all sincerity?" The wise thing to say on the phone is, "Have you had any cancellations?"

Try the bar

I tell people who don't have reservations to sit at the bar. The bar is a great place to eat, and I encourage it. And a lot of people who *do* have reservations end up sitting at the bar. People enjoy the action at the bar. It's not as formal. You get to hang out with different people, and often to try new things.

Do bribes work?

Our hosts are told to absolutely not accept cash. Whether they do it or not. . . . It's a capitalistic society, let's face it.

For those who would like to try, it's quite easy. Fold up a $20, $50, or $100 bill in a nice little package in your right hand, shake hands with the host or hostess, and say, "My name is so-and-so and I'd like a table."

There are some big restaurants here where you will not get a table without a reservation unless you give someone $100. It just ain't gonna happen. A $100 bill sometimes works miracles.

I don't discourage someone who has had a great time to

give the host a $20 tip on the way out. The host is the gate-keeper. People know when a host did his or her job and booked the room correctly. Plus, if you plan on coming back, that's a very good thing.

What about lying?

People regularly call up and say, "My name is Joe Smith and I have a reservation." We know they are lying. But you can't call the customer a liar; you have to be diplomatic. You say, "I don't see the reservation here, but let me see what I can do." It does put you in a funny situation. But we personally confirm every single weekend reservation.

31

HOW TO ORDER THE RIGHT DRINK CORRECTLY

Dan Rogan, professional bartender
As told to Douglas Trattner

About the Expert: *Dan Rogan has been a professional bartender for twenty years. He is currently the bartender at Classics restaurant at the InterContinental Hotel and Conference Center, Cleveland, Ohio's only AAA Five Diamond Award–winning restaurant.*

Before you can understand how to order a drink, you have to understand what it means to be a bartender. Doing the job right means learning on the job—and none of that Academy of Bartending stuff. Every time I see a graduate of one of those programs apply for a job, the bar owner typically tosses the application in the garbage. Those people usually end up teaching at the Academy. They have a vast knowledge of stupid drinks that nobody ever orders, and no people skills.

Bartending is 80 percent personality, 20 percent knowledge and skill. You can't learn personality at school.

First dates

At Classics we tend to get a very upscale clientele. We also get a lot of special-occasion customers—birthdays, anniversaries, and first dates.

First dates can be tricky because you don't want to look like a wimp, but you don't want to look like a lush, either. If a guy orders a strawberry daiquiri on a first date, chances are the

Big or small?

If you're looking to walk in, the size of your party really doesn't matter in getting a table. Sometimes deuces (two-seat tables) are harder to get than a four- or six-top. There is no true rule here.

The quieter nights in the restaurant business are Sunday, Monday, and Tuesday, and those are definitely the best nights to try to just walk up and be seated. As for times, we give everyone the same drill: Try 6:30 or 10 P.M. Everyone calls and asks for eight o'clock. I start laughing and say, "You really are kidding me, right? You're calling me on Friday night for a Saturday night reservation for eight P.M., and you're doing this in all sincerity?" The wise thing to say on the phone is, "Have you had any cancellations?"

Try the bar

I tell people who don't have reservations to sit at the bar. The bar is a great place to eat, and I encourage it. And a lot of people who *do* have reservations end up sitting at the bar. People enjoy the action at the bar. It's not as formal. You get to hang out with different people, and often to try new things.

Do bribes work?

Our hosts are told to absolutely not accept cash. Whether they do it or not. . . . It's a capitalistic society, let's face it.

For those who would like to try, it's quite easy. Fold up a $20, $50, or $100 bill in a nice little package in your right hand, shake hands with the host or hostess, and say, "My name is so-and-so and I'd like a table."

There are some big restaurants here where you will not get a table without a reservation unless you give someone $100. It just ain't gonna happen. A $100 bill sometimes works miracles.

I don't discourage someone who has had a great time to

give the host a $20 tip on the way out. The host is the gate-keeper. People know when a host did his or her job and booked the room correctly. Plus, if you plan on coming back, that's a very good thing.

What about lying?

People regularly call up and say, "My name is Joe Smith and I have a reservation." We know they are lying. But you can't call the customer a liar; you have to be diplomatic. You say, "I don't see the reservation here, but let me see what I can do." It does put you in a funny situation. But we personally confirm every single weekend reservation.

31

HOW TO ORDER THE RIGHT DRINK CORRECTLY

Dan Rogan, professional bartender
As told to Douglas Trattner

> **About the Expert:** *Dan Rogan has been a professional bartender for twenty years. He is currently the bartender at Classics restaurant at the InterContinental Hotel and Conference Center, Cleveland, Ohio's only AAA Five Diamond Award–winning restaurant.*

Before you can understand how to order a drink, you have to understand what it means to be a bartender. Doing the job right means learning on the job—and none of that Academy of Bartending stuff. Every time I see a graduate of one of those programs apply for a job, the bar owner typically tosses the application in the garbage. Those people usually end up teaching at the Academy. They have a vast knowledge of stupid drinks that nobody ever orders, and no people skills.

Bartending is 80 percent personality, 20 percent knowledge and skill. You can't learn personality at school.

First dates

At Classics we tend to get a very upscale clientele. We also get a lot of special-occasion customers—birthdays, anniversaries, and first dates.

First dates can be tricky because you don't want to look like a wimp, but you don't want to look like a lush, either. If a guy orders a strawberry daiquiri on a first date, chances are the girl's not going to be too impressed. Also, if he orders a beer, he isn't going to look very sophisticated.

A glass of red wine is a pretty safe and masculine way to go. You can also order a martini, as long as it's vodka or gin—but no specialty martinis. Don't ever ask for the martini list. Let the girl do that. (The only exception comes either with dessert or instead of dessert, where an espresso martini is perfectly acceptable.)

Any guy on a first date, or any other date for that matter, should remember that the only time it's okay for a guy to order a Cosmopolitan is when he is by himself, or maybe with his mother.

Martinis and the classics

The martini has been bastardized by many different ingredients. Nowadays, you can take any drink out there, put it in a martini shaker, strain it, and put it in a martini glass, and all of a sudden it's supposed to be a martini.

I am a fan, however, of all of the classic cocktails, which are making a bit of a comeback. Sidecars, Stingers, Manhattans, and Old Fashioneds have all had a bit of a resurgence. But those cocktails, which are based on darker liquors such as scotch and bourbon, came back into fashion when cigars became popular again. Even though both fads seem to be dying down, it's always appropriate to order one of these classic drinks.

Call your liquor

Some people always call their brand regardless of what cocktail they happen to be drinking. Women order Grey Goose cosmopolitans because they think that Grey Goose is the chi-chi vodka.

But if you're ordering anything that has juice in it, you're wasting your money because you can't taste the difference anyway. The only time I recommend ordering top-shelf liquor in a juice-based drink is when you plan on having a dozen of them. That way, your hangover won't be as bad.

If you order any liquor on the rocks, you have to call your brand. That is a definite rule of thumb. The same goes when you order something with just tonic or soda, and certainly with classic martinis.

But if you are ordering a single-malt scotch in an effort to impress somebody, don't order it on the rocks (i.e., the glass filled with ice) or with a splash of water, tonic, or soda. It should be drunk neat, or as close to neat as you can stand. The perfect way to order good scotch is with one or two ice cubes.

If you are going to order cognac, make sure you know how to pronounce it first.

Drinks for business

If you are having a drink during a formal or semiformal business meal (anything where you are not wearing jeans), vodka and tonic or gin and tonic are perfect choices, but make certain you order a top-shelf gin or vodka. Ordering a Tanqueray Ten and tonic sounds a lot better than saying gin and tonic. It sounds like you know what you're doing.

And never follow the lead of someone else. For instance, if your boss orders a glass of pinot grigio, don't say, "I'll have one, too." He'll know you're just kissing his ass.

Wines by the glass

Before the meal, it's safe to follow the season. If it's cool outside, red is appropriate. If it's warm outside, go with something white—but never zinfandel. Sweet wines are for women. Dry and full-bodied wines are best for men.

Cabernets are always a safe bet. Some wines that tend toward flowery, like a pinot noir, might come across as a little too feminine. And never ask for ice in your wine, white or red.

If you and your guest prefer two different wines, it's best to order glasses as opposed to bottles. But if you can find some common ground, it's nice to accommodate your guest so you can order a bottle. You can always hit your flask in the restroom.

Weddings and cocktail parties

White wine and vodka tonics are always safe, as is anything in a tall glass. You will also want something you can wrap a napkin around so your hands don't get too cold. Avoid martinis, which are difficult to walk around with. And remember that anything you set down will disappear, and then you have to get another drink.

Empty stomach

A glass of white wine is good if you're just starting out, as it will mix well with just about anything. If you start off with a stiff cocktail, such as a vodka drink, you can start getting your buzz on a little early and all of a sudden lose your appetite.

Trendy drinks

A Grey Goose martini up with blue-cheese olives is the drink du jour. It's the drink that everybody has to have. But men need to be cautious with this whole stuffed-olive craze. Men will order blue cheese– or anchovy-stuffed olives without taking into consideration what that will do to their breath. Fish breath won't get you too far with the ladies.

Dive bars

If you find yourself in a bar, rather than a restaurant or lounge, there's nothing wrong with a cold domestic beer. If you stick with imports, you'll get drunk much quicker. And no-body wants to make an ass of himself in a bar.

In addition to the fact that the wine selection usually sucks at a bar, you'll look stupid walking around with a wine glass when everyone else has a beer bottle.

If you're sauced

If you are getting drunk but don't want to look like a wuss, that's when you give the bartender the high sign. "Give me a vodka tonic (but make it all tonic), please."

A good bartender will play along and charge you accord-ingly. You want to be on your game, and you want to be able to drive home. There's no deal-breaker worse than driving a girl home and getting pulled over and tossed in jail.

Dinner parties

Picking a gift bottle for a dinner party can be tricky if you forget that it doesn't matter what the host will be serving for dinner, because the bottle you bring is technically a gift for the host and won't necessarily be served with the meal. A great bottle of single-malt scotch or a good bottle of red wine that they can age is always a great gift. If it's a business dinner, and you're looking for points, get a bottle of eighteen-year-old scotch. If it's just casual friends, a $20 bottle of California wine is fine. And remember to remove the price tag.

A drink for every occasion

Irish bar
    A shot of Jameson's and a pint of Harp.

Rock-and-roll bar
    A shot of Jim Beam and a Pabst Blue Ribbon tall boy.

Light beer

If you want to order a light beer, Amstel Light seems to have avoided the negative stigma of other brands.

Beer

It is also cool nowadays to really know your beers. Like ordering a Hoegaarden or a Hefeweizen. Stella Artois is a really hot beer right now. Cool beers might be the up-and-coming martini.

Super Bowl party

Beer is the only appropriate beverage. And never bring a six-pack; always bring at least a twelve-pack. And never bring dip.

32

HOW TO PICK THE PERFECT BEER

Julie Bradford, editor, *All About Beer* magazine

About the Expert: *A nationally known beer expert, Julie Bradford is the editor of* All About Beer *magazine and of allaboutbeer.com.*

Every guy should know how to enjoy beer. Enjoying beer can be a really simple thing. It doesn't have to be rocket science.

But what people miss out on is that there is so much more variety available than most people know. To enjoy beer more, it's important to know more about it, and to know the range of choices that are out there.

Find out what you like

The first thing is to figure out the types of beer that you like the best. The whole kingdom of beer divides into two big families: the ales and the lagers.

The fundamental division is based on the kind of yeast that ferments the sugar into alcohol. Basically, ales are fermented in warm temperature, and lagers are fermented in colder temperatures. I know that sounds kind of minor, a matter of a few degrees, but these two different kinds of yeast spin off different flavors.

For lagers, with the colder yeast, the resulting beer is much cleaner and has fewer side flavors. The flavors that you get from a lager tend to come entirely from the barley and the hops that are used.

In ales that are fermented in a warmer temperature (and

ready to drink sooner, by the way) the yeast throws off all kinds of other wild flavors. In an ale you'll get slight fruit flavors like peach and apricot.

The first thing that a brewer decides is, "Am I going to make an ale, or am I going to make a lager?" Ales are the traditional beers of England, the British Isles, and Belgium. The slightly newer family is the lagers, the traditional style of central Europe.

Lagers have gone on to conquer the world in the form of one kind of lager: the pilsner beer from Czechoslovakia. And it is that style that we have since modified. The big brewers have modified the pilsner style, and it is the great-granddaddy of all the mainstream lagers you find today: Bud, Miller, Coors, Becks, or Corona. Ninety-five percent of all the beer consumed in the world is descended from the pilsner style.

Try something else

Pilsner is a starter beer, but it is what most people finish with, too. The sad fact is that they leave behind as many as sixty or seventy other beer styles. The things that we are most familiar with in this country are the minority styles, but they offer an awful lot of flavor.

You should be sampling a lot of different styles. You may find one that you like more than the mainstream lager styles. You may find a bunch you like better.

How to find new beers to try

Pour yourself a small amount of Bass Ale and a small glass of Samuel Adams Boston Lager. Taste the ale and its fruity notes and then taste the lager, with its cleaner finish. Play with those two and think to yourself, I think I'm an ale man, or, I'm a lager guy.

The next thing that the brewer adjusts when making his beer is the balance between the dominant ingredients: malt and hops. Malt is the grain, malted barley: barley grains that have been germinated, and the germination has stopped with heat. The malt is where the brewer gets all the sugar to turn into alcohol.

The color of the beer comes from the malt and how roasted it is. Malt carries with it a bready quality. If a beer is described as malty, it's got a kind of biscuity, bready, toasty flavor to it. An out-of-the-oven flavor. It's grain.

Now, hops. Hops season beer. They were put into beer to balance the sweetness of malt. But how many hops you use, the kind of hops, and the way you use them determine whether you get a beer that leans toward the malt direction or the hop direction, aromas that smell like grass or flowers or grapefruit or cat pee. This is all possible. And you get a taste that can go from just a nice tang to it, all the way through a strong, bitter finish. If you want to try another two beers that are commonly available in order to figure out if you are a malt person or if you are a hop head try a Newcastle Brown Ale (more malty) and a Sierra Nevada Pale Ale (which is quite hoppy).

The final test is light beers vs. dark beers. People are often scared that dark beer is heavy or highly alcoholic, yet it is not necessarily either.

It is really fun to tell people that a Guinness has less alcohol and fewer calories than a Bud. Those are the two beers that I suggest trying side by side because they are both fantastic session beers (the term for a relatively low-alcohol beer that you are going to stick with all evening).

You can have several of them. If you don't want to be falling down drunk at the end of a night at the pub, these are good choices. Bud is very light malt. Guinness gets all its color from roasted barley.

Out of those three pairs, you should be able to say, "Well, broadly speaking, I prefer ales. I like malty beers and I kind of like dark beers." And you can go anywhere in the country and walk into an unfamiliar bar and get a recommendation from the bartender based on the styles you like. Another recommendation would be to drink local beers whenever you can. Go in and say, "What beers are made here in town?" And you can say, "I don't like hoppy beer; give me something malty."

Ask the bartender

The average bartender might not be very helpful, but if you go into a decent beer joint with some good selection, someone will know about beer. You could say, "I like a lot of hops. Who makes a good IPA?" and you can run into some great beers with local personality.

Another way to learn is to go to beer festivals. These are rare opportunities where for between $20 and $30 you can have an entire afternoon to walk around and sample different beers. The purpose of these events is to sample. You can come out of a good beer festival having tasted a range of good beer and discovered a new beer style you really like. Restaurants also offer tastings. If you go to a brew pub, they'll offer you a flight of beer, a sampling glass of each beer that they offer. Drink the beers from light to dark, and from lighter in alcohol and lighter in character to darker.

Should beer match food?

Beer doesn't have to match food, but if you don't try to make them match a little bit, you'll just lose out on the chance to enjoy your beer a little more. Mainstream beer is a perfectly agreeable thing to drink, but it's not necessarily the best beer choice for every food. I'd argue that beer is more versatile than wine when it comes to putting an alcoholic beverage with a meal.

No one has been quite as clear with the rules of beer as they have been with wines. Some have suggested that you treat ales as you would red wines and lagers as you would white wines. There is some truth to that, because lagers tend to be cleaner, but that tends to break down, because you can have some rather light ales and some really thumping lagers.

That is a good start. You can make parings that compare and contrast. Or look for similar characters or similar depths of flavor. For example, the really classic pilsners are wonderful with certain seafood. But they are also great with cream soups, where you have the clean edge of the pilsner and the creamy texture of the soup.

There are wine/food combinations that just don't work. Trying to find a wine that goes with any Asian cuisine tends to be a disaster. However, beer works well. And you don't have to drink just the mainstream styles that are brewed in Asian countries. You can cross cultures a little bit. I once had a good spicy Thai curry along with a pretty hefty India pale ale. It was particularly hoppy and they were just wonderful together.

A porterhouse steak was what was served in places where porters used to go to eat. The porter style of beer gets its name, apparently, from the appeal that this drink had for those people. And by golly, it goes very well with a steak because it is big, robust beer.

It would be a waste of pilsner to have it with a steak, which would overpower the beer. It would just disappear. Likewise, I'm not that big on conventional beer and pizza. If you really think about it, the combination of the sweetness and acidity of tomatoes just rolls right over the beer, unless you chose something with a little more oomph to it.

One thing that beer can do that many wines cannot is stand up to hearty desserts. Guinness and chocolate is a perfect fit.

Pay, pay, pay

When it comes to beer, pay for it. Pay for the best. Beer is an affordable luxury.

33

HOW TO SELECT THE PERFECT WINE

Paul Wagner, wine expert

About the Expert: *Paul Wagner is a faculty member of Napa Valley College in the Viticulture Department and gives lectures on wine all over the world.*

It is fascinating to me that people ask this question about wine, but they don't ask the same question about music. No one ever calls up a music expert and asks him, "What type of music should I like?"

There is an odd perception that there is a right and a wrong answer to wine, in a way that there isn't a right and a wrong answer to music, but that is not the case. I mean, my daughter likes different types of music than I do. I think she is crazy to listen to some of the things that she listens to, but there is no point in arguing. She's seventeen and I'm fifty-two and all we can do is occasionally hit on a Beatles song we both like.

More than red and white

I would say there are a couple of things more to it than just whether you like red or white. For most people who are unacquainted with wine, the bigger question is dry or sweet. Because if you decide that you don't like dry wine, then you just shouldn't bother ever trying red wines.

Almost all red wines are dry. I think there is a nice comparison here to people who drink tea or coffee. If you drink your tea or coffee without sugar, then you'll probably like dry wines. If you are the sort of person who uses two lumps rather than none, you should be looking at sweet wines, because that is probably a better match to your flavor profile.

The real point that you need to take home from this is that whatever you like is good, and don't ever let anyone tell you it is not. There are lots of different styles for lots of different people; why would you deny yourself the opportunity to try something new?

What goes with what

I'm not a big fan of the whole red goes with meat, white goes with fish thing. I prefer matching the wine to the color of the sauce. That solves the problem of what to do with pasta that might not have red or white meat in it. Pasta with clam sauce and butter—white wine. Pasta with tomato sauce, garlic, and anchovies—red wine.

Since most steaks come with red sauces, you go with red. Occasionally someone will serve hollandaise with a steak, but overall I think the sauce rule works well with steak. And it works for fish, too.

How to decide

If you don't know very much, trying to play the game of regions is almost certainly going to make you unhappy in the end because it is just too complicated. One of the more charming aspects of the wine industry is the practice of wine competitions, most of which are judged by pretty competent people.

If I were giving advice to someone who knew nothing about wine but just wanted to drink what were considered to be good, well-made wines, I would say go with high point scores, and go with metals.

Go to tastings

Go to tastings, if only to sort of learn the language the rest of the world uses to describe wine. So you'll go and someone will say that a wine tastes really tannin, and you'll learn what tannin is. (It is that really dry stuff in coffee and tea that's also in red wines.)

What do you buy for or order with other people? In a restaurant you have an advantage—you have a sommelier. I would say in a restaurant, in most cases, my sauce rule holds true. But you'll run into a problem when everyone orders something different.

Dry rosés and pinot noirs often match up with a lot of different things and are a very easy solution. But at a table like that, I would match everything up by the glass.

My wife and I order wine by the glass all the time, because we rarely order the same food. We sit down and instead of messing around with trying to find a bottle that will match with two completely different meals, we just order what works best by the glass.

Values

I would say that there are good values out there; for example, much of the wine from the Rhône Valley in France or from Rioja in Spain. Those are pretty good values. New Zealand makes very interesting white wines that are really good values.

I could get fired for telling you this, but everyone who had a really enviable reputation in the United States for making quality wine has come out with a less expensive version of that wine. It is called brand extension, and the wine is not as good. Robert Mondavi did it with Robert Mondavi Woodbridge.

Now everyone is doing it. That is why it is hard to order by label. A restaurant may have Kendall Jackson on the menu, but you don't know if it is the $30 good one, or the $6 cheap one.

You will also pay a premium for a wine from the Napa Valley in California over any other region in the United States. The Napa wines aren't that much better, but because people know that region, they will think it is the best, and pay for it.

So if you don't know wine, don't assume that more money buys you a better bottle. I would also avoid spending more than $30 on a bottle until you can really tell the difference. I would also avoid the Napa Valley; I would look at Monterey, Sonoma, and parts of Washington. Those are all places that make good wines.

How to store wine

All you have to do to store wine is pour it in a smaller bottle (so there isn't as much air), seal it tight, and put it in the fridge. It will keep for a week. You can use a wine stopper, but nothing works as well as putting the wine in a container just big enough and sealing it up. You could even use a pickle jar if you like.

Forget room temperature. Room temperature was a term that was coined in the 1800s to describe the temperature at which British people in their stately homes served their wines. Those were stone castles. It was damn cold in those rooms. The typical American home is too warm for wine. Wine is a beverage that should be refreshing. Simple rule: 60 degrees for red, 50 for white, and 40 for champagne. Those are all slightly too cold, but once they warm up in the glass, they will be perfect. There is nothing worse than pulling out a bottle of wine and letting it sit on the table as you are cooking dinner and then realizing that it is 75 degrees.

If you want to chill a wine in your fridge, twenty minutes for red wines, forty minutes for white wines, and an hour for sparkling wines. If you leave your wine in the fridge for a long time, the vibration of the fridge will muck up the wine. It won't happen in a day or two, but if you leave it there for a long time, the vibration breaks down the molecules in the wine and kills the fruit.

The best place for a wine rack is on the floor of a closet on an interior wall. The secret to wine is that it should be cool, but if it can't be cool it should be stable. Exterior walls get hotter and cooler during the day. Also, the more wine in the rack the better. The bottles can insulate one another. The worst place to put a wine rack is in the kitchen, or over the stove. You see a lot of beautiful built-in wine racks over stoves. The wine might as well be *in* the stove.

34

HOW TO WIN AN EATING CONTEST

Edward "Cookie" Jarvis, champion eater

About the Expert: *One of America's most successful competitive eaters, Ed "Cookie" Jarvis has won twenty-five title matches against some of the fiercest competitors this planet has ever seen. The thirty-eight-year-old has gained national fame for his gustatory feats, tackling a wide array of foods. Jarvis can polish off a large (seventeen-inch) pizza pie in three minutes flat. He also holds the record for vanilla ice cream, downing one gallon and nine ounces in twelve minutes. He also holds the world dumpling record—ninety-one in eight minutes. In 2004 Jarvis captured the World Rib Eating title at the Chinook Winds Casino in Lincoln City, Oregon. His Web site is www.hugeeaters.com.*

Some people may not believe it, but there is definitely a lot of training involved to win an eating contest. When I'm in training I sometimes drink a gallon of water in one minute. That really helps with the eating. Or I'll eat ten or twelve pounds of cabbage to stretch out my stomach.

I've done that [drinking] before major contests, including the cannoli contest [where Jarvis won by eating twenty-one cannolis in six minutes], but even after doing that, for a week after the contest you're still in pain. Those shells hurt going down because they are kind of hard.

Every food requires a different type of practice. My advice is to practice on that particular food so that your body is immune to eating whatever it is you have to eat. Try to get used to the taste. Some people don't like mayonnaise, but you better get used to it if you're gonna eat two pounds of it in thirty-five seconds, like I did one time.

I don't have a preference for a particular food when it comes to contests. They all have their own little challenges, as well as their fun aspects.

Hit the gym

I usually exercise in the gym five to six days a week. I'll ride the bike twelve to twenty-three miles a day. You want to physically train body parts; you want to keep everything in motion. People forget how hard it is to be a professional eater. You can't just be the guy who eats a lot, because you have to eat a lot in a short amount of time.

I'm actually on a diet right now. It pretty much consists of six egg whites and American cheese for breakfast. Then I'll have a few cans of tuna for lunch, and a normal dinner.

Practice, practice, practice

Don't practice by yourself. God forbid you choke without anybody there.

A lot of times I'll go to the buffet and eat twelve pounds of whatever they have for lunch. The average person won't do that. There are the grazers, and then there's me. After a while, the people there begin to notice what I'm doing and realize that I'm on a whole other level.

If you are going to get into professional eating, ease into it. Don't go into it full force or you'll get hurt.

I consult a dietician because I want to make sure I'm not putting myself in danger. I also get tested by the doctor every year to make sure everything's okay.

Get started

The first time I ever ate competitively, I did it as a publicity stunt for my real estate business. After a while I realized that this was my way into professional sports. Before I knew it, I was on ESPN and I was doing the Jay Leno show.

If you want to try it, start out small. Get started at the local wing joint before jumping into the big events. You don't want your first event to be the Wing Bowl, because you'll be blown away. But watch out for some of the smaller events. Not all of them have EMTs on-site, and that can get dangerous.

Not just one food

If you're going to be a competitive eater, you have to be ready for different kinds of competitions. The Battle of the Buffets is always hard. It consists of five contests over three days. You have to eat ten pounds of food per contest. That is a lot of work. If you are going to do that contest you really have to be strict with yourself. You never know what kind of food you'll be eating until you get there, so hitting the local buffet weeks in advance to practice on a wide selection of food is a smart idea.

If you don't like the food, you have to focus it right out. Use Vicks VapoRub to block out the smell. (Smell is the key. I can't tell you how bad cow brains and bull testicles smell, but I've eaten them both.)

The absolute worst thing to eat was mayonnaise. I was up against this guy who ate eight pounds. I ate four and could have eaten more, but I thought, This is terrible.

I have what I call the atomic shovel (an ice cream shovel), and it has won me a lot of contests. When I use that I can barely even taste the food. You do have to be clean about it or you risk getting disqualified. I once ate thirty-three ears of corn in twelve minutes and was pretty messy. You can't be a slob up there.

You also have to be prepared to travel if you're going to be a big-time eater. The bigger contests are spread out all over the country.

35

HOW TO SELECT AND COOK
THE PERFECT STEAK

Tiffany Collins, culinary director, Texas Beef Council

About the Expert: *Tiffany Collins is culinary director of the Texas Beef Council and has taught thousands of people how to cook beef in all its forms. She is a graduate of Texas Christian University and studied the culinary arts at Johnson and Wales University in Charleston, South Carolina. Tiffany has spent more than twelve years in the foods and entertaining industry working with Time Warner publications,* Southern Living, *and* Cooking Light *magazines.*

You need to determine your occasion before making a choice. Are you cooking for leanness? For elegance? For grilling?

A good rule of thumb that we use for beef is, if it ends in the word "loin," then it is going to be tender. For a lean cut, to save total fat, look at the round selection, like the eye of round or the top round. The most tender is the eye round.

You want to look for a steak that is well-marbled and a nice cherry red. That's pretty much it. And look for the same things no matter what cut of meat you are buying: Look for the color.

What do the grades mean?

There are eight quality grades for beef that can be assigned by a USDA grader, but only the top three are generally used by grocery stores and restaurants: prime, choice, and select. Factors considered by the grader are meat color, firmness, texture, age, and marbling.

Marbling is responsible for the flavor and juiciness of the meat. The more marbling present in the meat, the more flavorful and juicy the product. Therefore, the prime grade, which has the most marbling, is followed by choice and select.

Charcoal or gas?

When grilling, remember that charcoal is going to impart a different flavor altogether than gas. I find that half of my classes that I've taught here in Dallas were split in half in terms of which they preferred. I find that a lot of men like to play with fire, so charcoal is a good thing for them.

On the other hand, you have the ease of a gas grill. Again, each one will impart different flavors, so we highly suggest both. If you do go with the charcoal grill, we really do suggest that you don't just pile your charcoal. You want to build and layer your briquettes and saturate them in lighter fluid, or use a little chimney. That will provide an even cooking surface. You also want to make sure you let the briquettes burn until they are ashy before putting the meat on the grill.

How long will it last?

You can keep steaks and roasts in the freezer anywhere from six to twelve months. Ground beef will only keep for about three to four months in the freezer. You don't want to leave leftovers or other cooked beef in there for more than three months.

The fridge is different. Steaks and roasts will keep in there for three or four days, as will leftovers. Uncooked ground beef will only keep for a day or two.

Keep in mind that these guidelines are based on a freezer set at zero degrees and a fridge set between 35 and 40 degrees.

Purchase meats just before checking out at the supermarket and refrigerate them immediately in the meat compartment or the coldest part of your refrigerator once you're

home. When using frozen beef, defrost overnight in the refrigerator, never at room temperature. Wash your hands well
(twenty seconds) with hot soapy water before and after han-
dling raw meat and poultry.

Keep raw meat and poultry from coming into contact with
other foods during preparation. You should also wash all utensils, cutting surfaces, and counters with hot soapy water after
contact with raw meat and poultry. Never take beef off the grill
and return it to the same platter that held raw beef unless the
platter has been washed in hot soapy water.

Preparation tips

Marinating tips
1. Always marinate in the refrigerator, never at room temperature.
2. Marinating for onger than twenty-four hours can result in a soft
   surface texture.
3. Never save and reuse a marinade. If a marinade is to be used
   later for basting or served as a sauce, reserve a portion of it before adding the beef.
4. Allow ¼ to ½ cup marinade for each 1 to 2 lbs. of beef.
5. Marinate in a food-safe plastic bag or nonreactive container such
   as a glass utility dish.

Three easy steps to grilling beef
1. Prepare charcoal for grilling. When coals are medium, ash-
   covered (about thirty minutes), spread in single layer and check
   cooking temperature. Position cooking grid over coals. To check
   temperature, cautiously hold the palm of your hand above the
   coals at cooking height. Count the number of seconds you can
   hold your hand in that position before the heat forces you to pull
   it away; it should be four seconds for medium heat.
2. Season beef, straight from the refrigerator, with herbs or spices
   as desired. Place on cooking grid directly over coals.
3. Grill to desired doneness using a thermometer.

Tips on heat

Grilling at medium to medium-low temperatures ensures even cooking. If the temperature is too high, beef can char and become overcooked on the outside before the interior reaches the desired doneness. For best results, use an instant-read thermometer to determine doneness. For steaks and burgers, insert the thermometer horizontally into the side (not the top) to check the internal temperature.

1. Cook burgers to at least 160°F (medium doneness).
2. Cook steaks to at least 145°F (medium-rare doneness).

More good ideas

1. Rubs are a blend of seasonings, such as fresh or dried herbs and spices. They are used only to add flavor, not to tenderize. Apply rubs to the surface of uncooked steaks and ground-beef patties just before grilling.
2. Trim excess fat from meats to avoid flare-ups while grilling.
3. Use long-handled tongs for turning steaks; spatulas for burgers. A fork will pierce the beef, causing loss of flavorful juices.

Grilled Steak Santa Fe

Prep: 10 minutes • **Refrigerate:** 6–8 hours or overnight
Cook: 20 minutes • **Servings:** Serves 4

Ingredients:

1¼ pounds top round steak, cut 1 inch thick
6 tbsp. frozen margarita drink mix concentrate, defrosted
2 tbsp. chopped fresh cilantro
2 tbsp. vegetable oil
4 cloves garlic, crushed
2 tsp. ground cumin
½ tsp. salt
¼ tsp. pepper
1 large avocado, diced
¼ cup chopped red onion

1. In a small bowl, make marinade by combining margarita drink mix, cilantro, vegetable oil, garlic, cumin, salt, and pepper. Put 2 tbsp. of the marinade in a small container, cover, and refrigerate.

2. Place the steak and remaining marinade in a resealable plastic bag. Seal bag carefully and turn to coat steak. Refrigerate 6–8 hours or overnight, turning occasionally.

3. Remove steak from marinade and discard marinade.

4. Place steak on grid over medium, ash-covered coals. Grill uncovered for 16–18 minutes for medium-rare doneness, turning occasionally. Remove steaks and keep warm.

5. Just before serving, in a medium bowl, combine avocado, onion, and reserved 2 tbsp. of marinade mixture. Toss gently to coat.

6. Carve steak crosswise into thin slices. Serve immediately with avocado mixture.

36

HOW TO BEAT
AN ALL-YOU-CAN-EAT BUFFET

Hank Fraley, starting center, Philadelphia Eagles

About the Expert: *Hank Fraley is one of the National Football League's most unlikely stars. Having played his college ball at Division 1AA Robert Morris, Fraley's chances of getting an NFL tryout, let alone becoming the starting center for a Super Bowl team, were minimal. But, against the odds, Fraley accomplished exactly that, becoming a fixture on the offensive line for the Eagles.*

A lot of people go into a buffet thinking they are going to put it out of business, but then come out after eating only a couple of plates. If you really want to get the most out of a buffet, you have to prepare and pace yourself.

Buffet time should be reserved for the times when you are really, really hungry. It doesn't make much sense to go to a buffet right after having a snack. Maybe you've been working and haven't eaten anything since breakfast at 7 A.M. Now it's 7:30 P.M. and you're starving. This is when it's time to hit the buffet line.

It's like during training camp, when we make the rookies take us out to dinner. Now, we don't usually go to a buffet, but the way we do it, it looks like one. We get all the steaks and lobsters and side dishes. You name it, we order it.

The waiters bring out this enormous spread and the guys are like, "Whoa, that's a lot of food." We'll be there a few hours, easy. We're definitely stuffed when we hand the bill over to the rookies. That's important. We know we are going there to have a really big meal, so we make time for it. Don't head out to something like that if you are in a rush, because you won't enjoy yourself.

Yeah, we're going out because we're hungry, but we're also going out to have a good time. No one wants to speed through a meal, especially one where there are so many different things to eat. But then, you get really hungry after a day of training camp.

You have to take it easy, though. If you dive right in, you won't eat that much. We like to take our time. There's no rush; just sit back, relax, and enjoy the meal, no matter how big it is. We'll do that a couple times each season.

There are other times that food plays a part during the season. During the week while we're in-season, Donovan Mc-Nabb and I will stay late at the NovaCare Complex to watch extra game film of our upcoming opponent. We like to call it dinner and a movie. After grabbing some dinner from the coaches' buffet, we will lock ourselves in the QBs' meeting room, eating food and taking in the film, looking for defensive tendencies. Andy Reid likes to joke about Donovan continually feeding me cookies to keep me there late.

The same thing applies there. The food is a complement to the meeting, not the other way around. Look at it that way. If you are going out to a really big meal or a buffet, the food is a complement to the night out. You're there to have fun; if you are just focusing on eating a lot, you aren't having any fun. Most people who aren't having fun don't like to stay very long.

Be healthy

The nice thing about being with the Eagles is that we have nutritionists available to us. I realize that most people don't have that kind of personnel handy, but it makes sense to at least talk to your doctor if you are going to be making these really big meals a habit.

For us, we have to watch the types of food we eat. As a lineman, I can eat a pretty big meal, but I wouldn't want it to be made entirely of fried cheese.

I have to be careful because one of the great things about playing in Philly is the cheesesteaks. I usually get the "Whiz without"—a cheesesteak with Cheez Whiz and no onions—because I don't like onions. Back in Pittsburgh, I used to eat at Primanti Brothers'. I loved their hot Italian. There's sausage, cole slaw, cheese, tomatoes, and french fries, all in the sandwich. Those are big-time sandwiches. They're practically whole meals between bread. Just like eating a huge meal, you have to plan on eating those ahead of time. It's not a spur-of-the-moment thing.

Another thing to keep in mind is exercise. Sure, people look at football players and see really big guys, but we also work out on a daily basis. No one who hits buffets, or who just eats a lot, for that matter, should not work out. It's just not healthy.

Remember to talk with a doctor. I mean, every now and then going to a buffet or eating a really big meal like the one we make the rookies buy for us isn't that big of a deal. But if you want to make this the way you eat, you need to get checked.

37

HOW TO BUY CIGARS

James Yee, cigar expert

About the Expert: *James Yee is a cigar expert who writes for Allexperts.com. For the last ten years he has smoked an average of three cigars a day. He has also sampled all the major brands of Cuban cigars and is a recognized expert on them.*

With literally hundreds of different cigar brands and sizes currently available on the market, choosing a good cigar can be pretty overwhelming—not to mention confusing—for a novice cigar smoker. For beginners, the most crucial part when choosing a cigar would be selecting the right cigar strength.

Premium cigars can range anywhere in strength from mildly bland to high-octane powerhouses. For a novice, it's best to choose a cigar that is not too overpowering. Selecting a cigar that's too strong may not only sour your smoking experience, it would quite possibly make you ill as well.

Be strong, but not too strong

Some people like to stick to the old adage "taste is subjective." The strength of a cigar, however, is something that cannot be debated. Cigar strength is often the result of using a certain level of aged tobacco in the cigar.

A cigar is composed of three basic parts: the filler, the binder, and the wrapper. While the mild binder holds the cigar together and the aromatic wrapper provides a beautiful appearance, the filler is the heart of the cigar and contains a complex blend of tobacco that creates the cigar's distinct flavor. Based on the recipe, this is what defines how strong a cigar should be.

Looking good

With appearance, a cigar should always look good . . . good enough to eat. It's a known fact that consumers often purchase items based on aesthetics. People have an ideal color for their car, an ideal décor for their home, an ideal style for their wardrobe, and so on. Appearance is equated with quality.

It's no different with cigars. Although premium cigars are thoroughly checked by the factory's quality control before shipping, cigars do occasionally get damaged, grow mold, become over-humidified, or suffer bug infestations. Some of these rare occurrences are inevitable but, fortunately, avoidable.

When choosing a cigar, it's best to avoid cigars with any type of visible damage or suspicious-looking inconsistencies. Not only can a blemished cigar be unpleasant on the eyes, but these imperfections can actually impair the natural burn of a cigar when lit and ruin your enjoyment.

Size matters

For size, it's always best to pick a cigar that feels right for you. Much like a marathon runner will need the perfect shoe or a golfer must have the perfect driver, a cigar must also be right for the individual smoker.

A larger cigar may be more suited for a larger gentleman but may be uncomfortable to hold for a smaller man, and vice versa. It's best to choose a cigar that is not only comfortable to smoke but does not make you appear comical in the process.

In terms of dimensions, cigars are now available in hundreds of shapes and sizes. Though cigars are produced in many places throughout Central and South America, the United States, and Europe, cigars are all commonly categorized by shape and measured by length and ring gauge.

The length of a cigar is measured in inches and the ring gauge is the diameter of the cigar uniquely measured in 64ths of an inch. For example, a Double Corona measuring 8 x 49 would measure 8 inches in length, and 49/64th of an inch in ring gauge.

Ring gauges traditionally vary anywhere from size 23 to 52; however, newer shapes and sizes that are continually being created call for larger gauges. For countries that support the metric system, the measurements are often recorded in millimeters.

For shape, cigars are often sorted into two categories: *parejo* and *figurado*. Within these two categories are subcategories which further list cigars by name and size. *Parejos* are defined as the straight and more traditional-looking cigars that we're all familiar with and that range from 4 to 9½ inches in length. *Parejos* include such popular sizes such as the robusto, double corona, and Churchill.

Figurados are usually less traditional in shape and require more time and effort to create. These are the "odd-shaped" cigars. Though some may be rolled purely as a novelty, there are some *figurados* commonly smoked along with *parejos*.

Torpedoes, for example, feature a long cylindrical body with a tapered head. These resemble torpedoes (hence the name) and are favorite shapes among cigar smokers. Other *figurados* include football-shaped *perfectos*, double-tapered *diademas*, and bizarre-looking *culebras*. Spanish for the word "snake," *culebras* feature three *parejo* cigars uniquely braided together during production. *Culebras* can be smoked either individually or all at once.

Another classification for cigars is by wrapper color. During aging, the tobacco leaf can become darker and darker the more time it spends in the sun. In infancy, leaves generally have a mild green (*candela*) to light tan colour (*claro*); adolescent leaves will have a milk chocolate shade (*colorado*); and older leaves will have a reddish brown to dark chocolate appearance (*maduro*).

Leaves fermented for the longest amount of time possible will have a black color (*oscuro*). Most cigar smokers do prefer one type of wrapper over the others based on aroma and taste.

As a result, premium cigar brands are now offered in a variety of wrapper shades.

How much?

Price is often a concern, as people are unsure of how much to spend on a cigar. Premium cigars can range anywhere in price from $6 to $60, so for a beginner, it is always best to start out small and choose something that is not too expensive. Price doesn't reflect taste, so a regular $6 cigar can indeed taste just as good as a $60 limited-edition cigar.

With thousands of cigar brands on the market, it's up to the cigar smoker to sample as many brands as possible to discover the hidden, inexpensive gems.

Get started

Taking these points into consideration, a cigar novice should start with a mild- to medium-strength cigar that feels comfortable to smoke, is appealing to the eyes, and is not a strain on your wallet. By speaking with your local tobacconist, you may begin to explore the wide range of premium cigars and discover what is right for you.

38

HOW TO GET IN (OR BACK INTO) SHAPE

Mike Ryan, fitness trainer to the stars

About the Expert: *Fitness expert and personal trainer Mike Ryan has helped clients including Michael Jordan, Kobe Bryant, John Elway, The Rock, Kevin Spacey, and many others. Ryan has consulted on fitness for a variety of movies including* Fight Club, American Beauty, *and* The Scorpion King.

One of the first things I ask anyone is "What are your goals?" I'm a very goal-oriented person and I find it best to sit down with a potential client and get an idea of what it is they want to accomplish.

Take a picture of yourself before you begin your workout program. Then, as you reach certain goals and move along in the program, take more pictures. This way you can see firsthand just how much progress you are making. It is a lot easier to see the progress this way instead of just looking in the mirror every day. That really helps keep people motivated.

A lot of people, former athletes included, don't realize that they've let themselves go. So hanging the "before" picture on the fridge is a good idea.

Try everything

For people who are about to work out for the first time, and for former athletes, the best way to work out is to incorporate a little bit of both weight training and cardiovascular. You don't want to forget to work the heart out a little bit.

The big difference is the amount of time you put into the

workout at first. When I work with elite athletes we'll do an hour of weights and an hour of cardio, but for someone just starting out, you'll want to go with maybe thirty minutes of each and then work your way up to maybe forty-five. You don't want to overdo it, because that leads to injury.

And remember to stretch before and after working out and before going to bed.

Put in the time

The other thing people should know is not just how long to work out on any given day, but also how many days a week to actually get out there and do it. Those just starting out should do a three-day-a-week program, typically Mondays, Wednesdays, and Fridays.

That gives your body some time to recover for the next day's workout. Three days a week is okay, four is better, and five is just great. But again, if you've never worked out on a regular basis before, start slower. It really all depends on how much you can handle.

You are what you eat

Nutrition is huge. There are so many beliefs and philosophies out there, but I try to keep it pretty simple. While training, I recommend three square meals a day with two to three protein shakes as supplements. You want to be eating about every three hours. So maybe you have breakfast in the morning, then have a shake around ten A.M., lunch at three P.M., then another shake. You're constantly eating, but they are small meals. It keeps the body flushed.

When I'm working with someone, I allow one "cheat day" a week. I keep my clients under strict rules during the week, but when that seventh day comes up, it's all doughnuts and pizza.

I'm big on high protein. I believe that you should have one gram of protein for every pound of body weight. If you weigh

150 pounds, you should have 150 grams of protein a day. It's not that hard to do, either, because a typical protein shake has about 45 to 50 grams of protein in it.

I also don't buy into this whole "eliminate carbs" thing, but I do restrict carbs. Everyone reacts to carbs differently, but try to watch your rices and pastas.

Stick with it

I typically recommend sticking with a program for six to eight months and then taking a week off to reevaluate your goals. Take a picture to compare with your "before" shot. Use that as a guide. Maybe you're looking pretty good, but you want to hit your legs a little harder. Maybe you've gotten too big and you want to drop some weight and tone up.

Never too late

The great thing about the human body is that it remembers. So if you are someone who used to work out, your muscles will remember and react quicker. A well-trained body will respond better than one that has never worked out before and will allow for a more intense workout.

39

HOW TO LOSE WEIGHT

Richard Simmons, diet guru
As told to Sandra Carr

About the Expert: *Diet guru Richard Simmons created two of the most successful weight-loss programs ever: Deal-a-Meal and FoodMover. He has sold over 27 million units of his products over the past fifteen years, beginning with his* Sweatin' to the Oldies *infomercial, which debuted in 1986. Simmons has appeared on countless television shows including* Late Night with David Letterman, *where he has appeared regularly.*

The best way a guy can lose weight is to be good at math. It's all about math.

As a man, I have been fighting obesity and eating disorders my whole life. I was 200 pounds in the eighth grade and gradually ate my way up to 268 pounds when I graduated high school. I was not a sports-oriented guy. I was raised in New Orleans, which means that you're in hell's kitchen, just nothing but the devil's fried toys. Being in the middle of a city where Brennan's, Antons, and Arvos (mom-and-pop New Orleans–style restaurants) were all around caused me to have a very strong relationship with food.

I didn't count anything. I ate whatever I wanted to eat. I had baby fat and was supposed to lose it. Well, guess what? I didn't lose it.

Not just for women

I had eating disorders, which are mostly thought of as a woman's thing. But there are a lot of guys who are overweight who are not into sports and that sort of stuff, and who love food, like me. We have eating disorders, too.

I was throwing up by the time I was fourteen years old. I was taking up to thirty laxatives a day, and finally I starved. I went from 268 pounds to 119 pounds and ended up anorexic and bulimic in a hospital. At that point in my life, I had to decide: Did I want to live or did I want to die?

What was the best way? I had been overweight and I had been anorexic—so, how was I going to find my ideal weight, and how was I going to stay there? I tried the diets—the low this and the high that, the beach this, the Mediterranean, and the diet in the basement. I tried them all. And we [overweight people] try to take God's six food groups and eliminate them or say you can't eat this one with that one or you can't eat this one after seven o'clock. We restrict food, and that doesn't really make anybody happy.

The best way

When I decided to open my own exercise studio called Slimmons in Beverly Hills thirty-four years ago, people asked me, "What is the best way to lose weight?" And I always say it's the math.

There are life-insurance charts that tell you if you're this tall, if you're this short, if you're this old, if you're this blah, blah, then this is what you should weigh. You want to take that number and play with it a bit. So, if it says you should weigh 155 pounds, then you say, "Well, maybe between 150 and 160 pounds. I should be somewhere near there." And then, you start counting calories.

I didn't jump on the low-carb train or any of those ridiculous diets. If you take the word "diet" and break it up in syllables, the first syllable is "die."

I created something called the Deal-a-Meal: I cut out little pieces of construction paper. The red ones were the protein cards and the yellow ones were for fat. You would get a certain amount of the cards per day and when you moved them over in your wallet, you knew what you ate, and you stayed within your calories.

Then I created the FoodMover, which went into an address book with little windows. So, when you ate an apple you pulled down a fruit window; when you ate three ounces of chicken, you would pull down three protein windows. What I tried to do is say, okay, you're supposed to eat X-amount of calories a day. Let's say that it's 1,600–1,800 calories. In order to lose or maintain weight, you then have to figure out how many calories you have to burn.

Exercise

People say to me, "Richard, how many times a week should you exercise?" And I always ask, "How many days a week do you actually eat?" The answer is seven.

We're still looking for the magic bullet—the surgeries that have done so much today for people to lose weight, for example. The shots, the pills, and the infomercials that sell quackery on television. If you ate 500 extra calories that day, you know what? You're going to have to burn 500 calories.

Attend an aerobic class, walk, or strength train. The day you don't exercise is the day that you really have to do the math and say, "How many fewer calories I should eat in order to stay at this weight?" You really need to do the math. I eat 1,600 calories and 30 grams of fat a day.

By exercising an hour and fifteen minutes a day, my weight remains at 148 pounds. The day you overeat or exercise less is the day you gain weight. So, basically, that's the math of it.

Like yourself

Now, there's another part of it. The math is fine for you to understand how many calories and fat grams you're eating and how many calories and fat grams you can work off to stay at your ideal weight. But none of that makes sense, nor will it happen unless you do the first thing: The first thing is liking yourself.

Unless you have high self-esteem and can get yourself to eat healthy and exercise every day, you will always battle your weight. You have to give yourself compliments every day. You have to look into a mirror and say, "I'm worth it. I'm really going to do this. This is one of my projects. I'm going to make this commitment and I'm never going to give up. I'm going to do this day in and day out and be the best that I can be."

People who are having trouble with their weight are having trouble with their self-worth and their self-esteem. The bottom line is, you have to like you. I don't care what you weigh, I don't care how much money you make, and I don't care what kind of car you drive. You have to look frankly into the mirror and love what God gave you. Because if you don't love yourself each and every day, you will not love yourself enough to make great food choices. And you will always hear the negative voices in your mind that are telling you that you will never do it.

40

HOW TO SPEAK IN PUBLIC

Joe Tait, play-by-play announcer for the
Cleveland Cavaliers

About the Expert: *Joe Tait, the radio voice of the Cleveland Cavaliers basketball team, regularly delivers a program titled* From MC to the NBA in 25 Easy Steps *to college students. Tait's numerous awards include Sportscaster of the Year in 1974, 1976, 1978, 1991, 1996, and 1999.*

I never had any fears or reservations about making this my career, but public speaking can be a challenge for anyone. If you're self-conscious one of the old tricks that actually works is to imagine your audience in their underwear. Or, pick one person out of the group and act like you're talking only to him or her.

Eye contact is always good. No one wants to see a speaker who is always looking down at a stack of note cards. Don't, however, look over the audience. A lot of people try that old trick. Shift your gaze and look at a lot of people. Make people interested in what you are saying.

Once you've begun to talk, you can get to know your audience and play off them.

Don't forget the audience

My public speaking gigs are a little different from the games I do on the radio because, for one thing, you can see the audience. You get an immediate reaction.

I was invited to deliver a sermon recently. I had never done that before and wasn't sure how to approach it. I went there and inserted some humor. People were laughing, and the pastor was impressed. "I never thought of using humor," he told me, but after seeing me he decided to incorporate it into his sermons on a regular basis. Going into it I was surprised that the stained-glass windows didn't blow out when I walked in.

The key is to pick up on the mood of the audience. If you have a particularly bad audience there isn't much you can do other than plug away with what you have. You have to be ready to ad-lib based on the mood of your audience. Doing games on radio is all ad-libbing, so I've had a lot of practice. You don't know what is going to happen. You just have to paint the picture in an interesting way.

Most of the good stuff is spontaneous. "Wham with the right hand" [Tait's signature call] just came out after Hot Rod Williams came up with a big dunk one night. Everyone back at the station said they loved it and I should work it into the shtick. Then I listened to the tape and thought, Yeah, that sounds pretty good.

It works like that sometimes in front of an audience. You think you're just doing an all right job when someone tells you you just said something great, then you realize that when you play it back. You never know when a gem is going to come out.

Be prepared

By far the best piece of advice I can give someone about speaking engagements is to practice everything, but especially tough names. Say them over and over again. For several years Vitale Potapenko was playing center for the Cavaliers, and the pronunciation I was given was "Pot-A-Penko." I was using that pronunciation, the public address announcer was using it—we all thought that was how you said his name. Then after a few months his parents came to a game and couldn't figure out why we were all mispronouncing their son's name. That's when we found out it was "POTa-Penko." It gets tough like that sometimes, especially with the big influx of European talent in the NBA.

When you get good, though, you have to be careful not to be overconfident. Then you get to floundering. It's like when a pitcher gets a little cocky and thinks, I've got these guys by the balls. Six homers later you're in the showers.

If it's not going well, switch topics or move ahead in your material to get the audience back. If they're hitting your fast-ball, switch to a curve.

There is no such thing as a perfect speaker. If you're good, you can get away with murder and people will still like you. The trick is to roll with the punches and learn from your mistakes.

41

HOW TO GET A MASSAGE

Christopher Hall, massage therapist

About the Expert: *Christopher Hall graduated from the Desert Institute of the Healing Arts in Tucson, Arizona, one of the top massage schools in the country, in 1999. He currently works at Tirra Salon and Day Spa, an Aveda spa near downtown Chicago.*

A lot of people don't realize that men can come in and get facials and massages. We don't check the genitals at the door, but men tend to have a lot of issues when receiving a massage.

When you do go for a massage you should expect a lot of professionalism. You should expect it to be very clean, very quiet—a calming room. The massage therapist will also have a willingness to work with you and within your boundaries. Sometimes people don't feel comfortable removing their underwear. Other people do.

What (not) to wear

How to dress is pretty standard. I think that most people would say that if you want to keep your underwear on, it is okay. Any time I talk with new clients, especially male clients, I tell them that they can leave their underwear on if they want. If they are comfortable taking it off, that is okay, too.

When I have clients who have issues in their hips, I tell them that it is easier to work that region if they take off their underwear. You can do some work on the hips, or glutes, through the clothing, but it is not nearly as effective.

Some people may find it awkward when their therapist is of the opposite sex. People just need to realize that therapists are professionals. It is just like going to your doctor.

You may be a little embarrassed by some things, but the person who is working on you has seen that and much worse. Massage therapists look at the session as though your body is here and it needs work. It doesn't go any further than that.

They've seen bigger, too

The client also needs to remember that if he does get an erection it is not considered sexual. We understand that we are moving a lot of fluids around the body, and it is also pretty intimate touch. In our society men don't get touched that much, so any kind of touch might trigger that response.

If it does happen, he can always ask for a towel. But remember that the client shouldn't make a big deal about it, and the massage therapist certainly shouldn't make a big deal about it, either.

Trust your gut instinct. If you are uncomfortable, the massage has gone too far. If you're feeling that something is a little off, it's gone too far. Most places have a rule that wherever the drape, towel, or sheet ends, that is where the boundary is. And any genitalia touching is going way too far. Any place that has licensing will have those rules.

A massage is actually a very valuable therapeutic tool that will help your body. More people are going to be aware of this now that more and more insurance companies are covering massage therapy.

There is kind of a debate about that in the massage community. There are people like me who think that it is great because it increases the availability of massage, and its validity as a therapy. People are also worried that the insurance companies will then control the cost of it. So it is a double-edged sword.

Who should get a massage

Most people are good candidates for a massage because of the amount of stress that we put ourselves through. We are also poorly aware of our bodies and how badly we abuse them. A lot of people don't realize the physical impact stress has on the body and how it seriously impedes the functioning of the immune system.

Make sure that you wear loose, comfortable clothing, and other than that, just enjoy it.

42

HOW TO NEGOTIATE

Reed Bergman, sports agent

About the Expert: *Reed Bergman is the chief executive officer of Playbook Inc., a sports marketing firm. He has worked with a large list of superstars, including Barry Bonds.*

How you prepare for a negotiation depends on what type of negotiation you are conducting. First of all, everyone has a different negotiation style. Some folks take a more cerebral approach and some folks like to do business based on relationships.

At the end of the day what you really have to do is bury yourself with qualitative analysis. And again, depending on what type of negotiation you are in, you have to have comparisons and statistics. You have to have different scenarios under which certain situations will play themselves out.

I think there are a lot of keys, but preparation is certainly a critical success factor in the process. You obviously need a good command of your subject matter to be successful. You also have to be passionate about your product. If you're not passionate about your position or product it will show.

How much is about money?

Whether you take every dime on the table or worry about how to protect the relationship going forward depends on the situation. There are certain scenarios where you will examine the climate.

If you're talking about an athlete and their salary or contract, ultimately you really want to make sure that the lifestyle for that player is going to be the best possible quality of life. It depends on certain circumstances, but you may wind up taking less money in a certain market because the quality of life is going to be better or the team is going to be more competitive.

There are so many circumstances that each negotiation has to be specifically tailored to your product. You can't just negotiate in some kind of vacuum. You have to really understand the personality you're dealing with. You're representing somebody and must make an intelligent decision on what is the best of all possible scenarios for this person.

Bad negotiators

I deal with people all the time who think a negotiation has to go a certain way, otherwise they haven't been successful. The most successful negotiations are the ones where you feel like you may not have gotten everything you wanted. The other guy feels the same way, but you feel that you're comfortable with the solution.

To me, something about arbitration in baseball is a very unnatural process because teams have to say negative things about their player. Many times the player will listen to all the things the team can find wrong with him, and it is a potentially hard resentment.

Every agent has a different style. I would say that some agents like the arbitration process because it can potentially allow you to maximize dollars for your client, but there can be psychological ramifications. If the player is not able to handle hearing negativity in the process, you're better off avoiding arbitration.

What to avoid

The biggest mistake I see regularly is when it becomes this kind of scorch-the-earth tactic. I've always been a believer that you catch more flies with honey than you do with vinegar. I like to do things based on relationships, and I think sometimes you'll find the person on the other side of the table takes the position that will ultimately cause animosity. That's not always a good negotiation.

I find this to be true in every single capacity of life. Dealing with your teacher, your girlfriend or your wife, your children, or drive-through window attendants—everything is a negotiation. This doesn't mean they all have to be dramatic, but the way we communicate is in many respects a negotiation.

The hardest negotiations that you're ever going to have is negotiating for yourself. Whether it's your career or anything else, representing yourself is the reason why somebody like me is in business. You can't really be an advocate for yourself. Negotiating for yourself can get too emotional.

43

HOW TO CHANGE YOUR OIL

Memo Gidley, race car driver
As told to Marshall Pruett

About the Expert: *An accomplished race car driver, Memo Gidley can currently be seen driving Ten Motorsports Riley-BMW V8 Daytona Prototype with co-drivers Michael Mc-Dowell, Michael Valiente, and Jonathan Bomarito in the Grand American Rolex Sports Car Series.*

Changing your oil is a straightforward affair. The act of changing it can be fun, but be prepared for an absolute mess if you don't prepare ahead of time. Washing oily hands is easy; an oil-stained driveway never goes away.

My dad showed me how to change oil in a car when I was a little kid, way before big auto stores popped up on every corner. Now, all you need to do is go down to a Pep Boys store or a NAPA, tell them exactly what kind of car you need to change oil in, and they'll give you everything you need.

What you need

This makes life so easy—you don't have to know anything about what you need to get the goods for an oil change. Walking in and giving the brand, model, and year of your car will help them to supply you with the exact oil filter and oil you need.

You need to have an oil-filter wrench, an oil drain pan, some rags, and a container to put the used oil in. If you are really smart, you'll buy a few latex gloves to keep yourself as clean as possible.

Once you've paid for your equipment and gotten back home, you have a couple of options on how to change your oil (it depends on the type of car you have, and how old it is). Most older cars—anything before the '90s—won't have any sort of protective pan beneath the engine bay. If your car does have one, you'll have to remove it to drain the oil. This is never fun. I once cut a six-inch round hole in the pan on a car I had just so I could drain the oil without having to crawl on my back to take the dang belly pan off.

To get the pan off, a jack and two jack stands will be needed. Jack up the car from the front. Place the jack under the lower front crossmember. That's the metal piece beneath your engine and the lower front suspension bolts. It's very beefy, and is a perfect location to jack your car up from.

With the front of the car up high enough to put the jack stands in place, put them on the outer edges of the crossmember, just before the point where the suspension connects. Make sure they are solidly in place and have good contact with the car before letting the car down. Doing this properly is the most important aspect of changing your oil, because you don't want the car to fall on you.

Now you are ready to remove the belly pan. It's usually only a few screws, so a screwdriver of some sort will be required. With the pan off, find the oil drain plug, located on the bottom of the engine—it's never in the same place from one car to the next. Once you've found the plug, you'll also need to determine what type of socket or wrench you'll need to remove it. There are many different types.

Once you've found the proper wrench/socket to remove it, have your oil catch pan and a few rags close by. Break the plug loose (it will usually take a bit of effort—those things need to be tight), but don't unscrew it all the way. Put the oil pan directly beneath the drain plug hole and start unscrewing it the rest of the way.

The plug will likely have an o-ring or a seal that goes between the plug and the hole. Do not let the o-ring fall off the plug and drop into the pan. When you pull the plug and o-ring away, there will always be a strong stream of oil that wants to shoot out. Try to use the plug to block the hole halfway to slow down the surge of oil coming out.

Once the oil has finished draining (you don't have to wait until there is absolutely no oil coming out), put the plug back in, making sure it's on tight.

Halfway there

You are only half finished at this point; replacing the oil filter is next. Find where it is and position the oil drain pan beneath it if possible. Place three or four rags beneath the oil filter to catch the inevitable splash of oil that will come out. Draining the oil from the plug can be done cleanly most of the time; changing the filter is where things get messy.

Use your oil-filter wrench to unscrew the filter (counterclockwise to remove, clockwise to put it back on), and be prepared to tip the threaded part of the filter up once you have it off the car. This will prevent oil from spilling out. Place the used filter in your catch pan and allow it to drain. At this point, clean up any oil drips or spills from the old filter that are in your engine compartment and get ready to put the new filter on.

I always prefer to pretreat the new oil filter by slowly pouring a quarter of a bottle of oil in before screwing it into place. Since we've drained all the oil from the engine, the new oil filter will be bone dry when we start the car back up again. Even if it's only for a split second, I hate thinking that my engine might not have oil being circulated—and a dry oil filter will allow this to happen until all the new oil can circulate.

With the new filter on and tightened, you are ready to fill the car up with the rest of the oil, and then you're done. Find the oil cap, unscrew it, and use a funnel to add your oil.

After adding the suggested amount called for by your car maker, put the cap back on and let it all settle for a minute or so. After it settles, check the oil dipstick to be sure your oil level is close to the MAX line on the stick. Start the car and let it run for a minute or so (don't rev it, just let it idle). The oil will fill all the hard-to-find spots in the engine, and the oil level (on the dipstick) will come down just a little bit. Turn the car off and check the oil level again. If you need to, add a little bit (usually not more than a quarter of a one-quart bottle) to bring the oil up the MAX line.

Cleaning up

You're done with the car, but have one last thing to do. You've got five plus quarts of dirty oil and an old oil filter you need to dispose of. Pour the oil into a sealable container, and put the oil filter into a couple of sealable Ziploc bags (use a couple to make sure it doesn't leak). The same store you bought the new oil and filter from can also probably dispose of these for you. Whatever you do, don't dump the oil in the garbage or down a drain—a single drop of oil will pollute one million gallons of drinking water.

44

HOW TO PIMP YOUR RIDE

Q, manager, West Coast Customs

About the Expert: *Q is the manager of West Coast Customs, a "full custom" auto shop featured on the MTV show* Pimp My Ride.

We're a full custom shop, so our average client spends about $30,000 to $50,000. We had a guy come in here recently and spend between $150,000 and $200,000 in one trip. It's not your average shop. When you come to West Coast Customs, you're getting the full shot.

Do it yourself

You could purchase some stereo components, head units, and equipment like that.

You could also get a rim and tire package.

Make sure to get it already mounted and balanced, and then you can put it on yourself. It's not very complicated at all to put rims on your car. All you have to do is take off the old ones and slide the new ones right on. It's pretty much like changing a tire.

If you're a total novice and you want to change your car's appearance, I'd probably recommend what they call a vinyl wrap kit. This is basically a big sticker that goes around the whole car (or you can get it cut up). People will think your car is professionally painted, but you can get these kits for as little as $1,500. It's pretty easy to put on, too. Just stick it on and smooth it out, and you're ready to roll.

You do the doors

Lambo doors—where the front doors open up and toward the front of the car, similar to the way the doors open on a Lamborghini Countach—are pretty easy to put in. Suicide doors, which open opposite each other, can also be simple. With these, the door handles are right next to each other. The locking mechanism is in the center of the door area.

On some car models, these things can be done simply by repositioning the hinge. On others you're going to have to do a lot of fabrication to make it work. That includes fabrication on the body of the car, on the hinge itself, and sometimes on the door as well. With the Lambo doors, all you need is the hinge kit. There are several manufacturers of the Lambo door kit, and someone who has experience working on cars can get one door done in about four hours. So you could get the whole thing done in one workday if you wanted to.

Leave it to the pros

Putting TVs in the headrest is pretty complicated, and I would only recommend that you get it done by a professional. If you don't know what you're doing, you're probably going to end up buying a new headrest, and that can get expensive. It's more involved than just cutting holes and putting TVs in there. When you want a clean install you have to build a ring, which involves some woodshop tools, like a table saw and a router, to build the ring that goes around the monitor so that it looks flush. And that is what actually holds the monitor in place. It's a lot more complicated than just throwing in a new head unit up front.

Another thing you can do yourself is put a PlayStation in. They now have kits now that make it as simple as plugging the unit into the cigarette lighter. You don't even need the monitors to be preinstalled. Just buy what's called a travel pack.

Be careful

The one thing I always tell my customers when they are "wet behind the ears" is that the car will never be the same. Sometimes it'll be better, but it's never the same. I'll take their whole car apart and they'll notice something that might be a little off.

You also have to be careful about the impact on your insurance of any changes you make. A lot of times you have to get appraisals, and you have to get aftermarket insurance. That's going to compensate you in case of a theft, because normal insurance won't cover a lot of the work that we do.

There was a case in which we were sued by the DMV for taking a steering wheel off, removing the air bag, and putting a TV monitor in. But what we learned was, if the client had taken the steering wheel off and then turned it over to us for the install, we would have been fine. The client has to take the steering wheel off himself. I cannot take it off or disengage the air bag. They have to do it themselves, and then bring the car to me.

How to insure your "pimped" car

Robert V. Gay Jr., owner of two Nationwide Insurance branches

As far as auto insurance is concerned, there are two definitions of altering your vehicle. One is called a customized vehicle and the other is called an altered vehicle. A customized vehicle is a vehicle that has cosmetic, or non-performance-related, modifications. Examples include custom paint, decals, mirrors, graphics, seating, upholstery, carpet, and other aftermarket accessories such as chrome or magnesium wheels. If you are going to do anything like that to your car, you, as a car owner, have to contact us and provide us with the documentation of how much that customization is worth. Then an appropriate increase in premium is charged for the additional amount.

An altered vehicle is a vehicle that has been significantly modified from the original manufacturer's specifications for the primary purpose of increasing its performance. That is what we call "souping up" a car, one with oversized tires or oversized cylinders, for example. Most standard insurance companies will not insure that type of vehicle, though insurance is available on the specialty market.

So that is kind of how that works. But the ones that are "souped up" almost become specialty products, and you have to go to those particular carriers that will write that policy, and that is a lot more expensive.

If you don't do anything, all the insurance company is going to cover is what a normally equipped car would cost. It's exactly as though you are putting $10,000 worth of stereo equipment into your car. You need to have an endorsement on your policy that would cover that, because most cars come with much less expensive radios.

45

HOW TO GET ON A REALITY SHOW

Mark Cronin, producer, *The Surreal Life*

About the Expert: *Television producer Mark Cronin currently produces* The Surreal Life *on VH1. He previously produced MTV's* Singled Out *and a number of other shows.*

Reality shows are all very different. Obviously, *The Surreal Life* is celebrity-based, so there's no way to get on it unless you're a celebrity. *Singled Out* was based on kids, so we used to go out and pick them up off the beach. We had a recruiting department that used to fan out. I'd bet about half of our staff was made up of recruiters, because we needed a hundred kids a day.

To be completely honest with you, if I wanted to be on a show like *Singled Out*, I would live in California, because none of those shows really do national searches. They just recruit locally.

They may go as far south as San Diego and as far north as San Francisco, but that's about it. And that's also true of shows like *Blind Date* and most lower-budget game shows that are shot in L.A. They mostly look for contestants locally because they don't have travel budgets—not for their recruiters, and not for the contestants.

So my first word of advice for anyone who wants to be on those types of shows that is you have to live in this area.

And then the second word of advice is, you've got to be good-looking. One of our biggest concerns on MTV's *Singled Out* was that we wanted all of the kids to be really attractive.

Read the papers

The bigger reality shows—the big national network shows like *The Apprentice*—do real national searches. There are often local cattle calls where they'll ask people to come down, much like *American Idol* does. They all advertise; there are many local newspapers to check to see if recruiters are going to be coming through your area.

Be honest

Producers are looking for people who are willing to be very honest on-camera. That's one of the most common things. You want people who can speak their feelings very clearly. It's one of the most important traits of reality-show stars.

If someone's not very articulate, or if they are unwilling to say how they feel, if they get mad at somebody and they internalize it, it's very bad television. So one of the primary things that the types of shows—like *Big Brother*—that put contestants together in a house are looking for is interaction between the characters. Not only are they looking for big personalities and colorful personalities, they're also looking for very articulate people who are not afraid to say how they feel.

Not everyone is good at it. My advice would be, if you want to get noticed out of the thousands of people the producers are going to look at for any particular show like *The Bachelor* or *The Bachelorette* or *Big Brother*, is to be very, very forthcoming. They want people who will say how they feel or tell somebody that they don't like them, or will laugh out loud at a joke.

Don't be shy

Shy doesn't work. And to be honest with you, many people who want to be actors are not forthcoming with their feelings. It takes a different kind of person.

The person who wants to become an actor wants to play a

part or play a character or wants to have a script, a set of lines from which they can portray a certain set of feelings. But they don't want to externalize their own personal feelings. And very often actors are not very articulate. Many, many great stage and film actors are not very articulate. They do really well with scripts, but they're not the type of people who tell good stories.

Reality TV is not a gateway to acting. There are some reality shows that look for actors, like *The Starlet* and *The Next Action Star,* and I suppose that's the aim of the thing. But if you want to be an actor, don't go do *The Apprentice*, because you won't get on. It's a business show, and the people they are looking for are not people who play characters, they're people who are interesting, colorful characters themselves. It's a completely different world. This is a good route, however, if you want to get into hosting. It's good training for speaking off the cuff with a microphone in your hand. But it is not good training for an actor, and it is certainly not indicative of how you'll do as an actor.

If you don't look good

There's not much you can do about your looks. I would do everything I could to look good. I would do everything I could to be very, very, very personable and appealing.

If you are a reasonably good-looking, likable, and appealing person, the biggest thing you can do to stand out is to be extremely articulate. Tell good stories and joke with the producers directly. If there is something interesting in the room or there is something shocking you can say about the producers, go for it. You have nothing to lose. Anything you can do to get noticed is good.

Being outrageous helps. You see it on *American Idol*, but they are looking for good singers. You can go show up in a Bozo outfit and they'll use you on the show, but you won't advance anywhere, which is fine if that's what you're after.

Most shows are out for something particular. On *The Apprentice* they're looking for real business drive and savvy, high energy level, and a lot of good ideas for business.

On *The Bachelor* they're looking for people who sincerely are looking for an emotional attachment and have come to this TV show to try to find it. Do your homework on the show you want to get on.

They really like you

Likability is a huge thing. Very rarely will someone who is not likable get cast. Once in a while, or once in a show, they'll try to cast someone who is outrageously unlikable, but for the most part, the bulk of the cast is made up of people who are likable.

I don't know how to tell someone to be likable. It's a hard one. You either have it or you don't, but that is what the producers are looking for—people who the rest of the country won't mind having in their living room once a week.

It does, however, help to be one of the reality show stereotypes, like "extreme bitch." It helps to be more extreme than even-keeled. A friendly guy, anybody who is right down the middle, probably won't have much of a chance. Whatever it is that you think you are, push it up a little bit when you're in the room or making your tape. Try to find that character inside yourself and get it out.

46

HOW TO PICK A MOVIE

Leonard Maltin, movie critic

About the Expert: *Recognized as one of the leading authorities on movies and moviemaking, Leonard Maltin has become a household name and media personality thanks to his regular appearances on the highly successful syndicated TV program* Entertainment Tonight *and his daily radio feature,* Leonard Maltin's Radio View.

What are you in the mood for? There are times you just don't want to see something heavy or serious. And there are other times when you want to be challenged (though some people are never in that mood). And sometimes it is that indescribable something that makes a film sound intriguing or appealing. If I knew what that X-factor was, I could be a very wealthy man.

Some people put their faith in critics, and some people put more faith in the guy standing next to them at the water cooler or the woman they strike up a conversation with in their doctor's waiting room. Either one is valid.

If you listen to critics, it's probably because you align yourself with a particular critic. You know that his or her tastes tend to reflect yours. The reverse works, too: If certain people like a film, you'll hate it, and vice versa.

One of the imponderables is the films that critics love, but the public doesn't. It happens all the time that there are films you can't pay people to go see, and it is sometimes hard to understand why. Of course, there are also movies that critics hate but audiences love. I wouldn't have predicted a *Friday the 13th Part 2*, let alone a part 10.

Do critics matter?

Major Hollywood movies are more bulletproof than are smaller films, which benefit much more directly from critical support. There were two small success stories at the time of this writing: *March of the Penguins* and *Mad Hot Ballroom*, both films with modest advertising budgets that were entirely dependent on good reviews and strong word of mouth.

Art houses give movies more of a chance in some ways. They're not as anxiety-prone as the big boys, but they also can't afford to subsidize a movie that isn't earning its keep for very long. But the people who run those theaters have better antennae, I think, than a lot of the big boys. They can tell when something is building, even if it's building slowly. They have more patience and faith in certain films.

Of course, if you don't live in a major city, finding those films can be a problem. That's why it's such a shame that Robert Redford didn't follow through on his idea to start a chain of Sundance Cinemas. It was a great idea.

I absolutely think there's an audience for that type of filmhouse.

I teach a class at USC, and only a quarter of the 360 students are film majors. Some of them take it because it's an easy couple credits. I have found to my great pleasure that if you give people a chance and help them understand what they're about to see, they reach further than you might expect.

These are young people who for the most part would rather have a root canal than read subtitles, but then I show them *City of God* and have the filmmaker there in person, and they love it.

Experiment

Try something different. You might not like it, but maybe you'll discover something new. That's what happened with a lot of people who went to see *Crouching Tiger, Hidden Dragon*. Many of these people had never seen a subtitled movie before, and had never seen an Asian movie before, and it was kind of a breakthrough.

There are people who possibly never spend money at a box office to see a documentary who go to see Michael Moore's films. But the audience for documentaries is growing because the documentaries are entertaining and people are responding.

Sometimes people go to see a film that they otherwise wouldn't have because of really strong reviews or word of mouth. But there's a catch: Every year there's a film that gets too much praise. By the time people see it they have outsized expectations for what may be a very small-scale film. *Sideways* would be one. The year before it was *Lost in Translation*.

My theory is that everything has to do with expectations. Everything about your reaction to a movie has to do with your expectations going in. Every film is different.

47

HOW TO SURVIVE ARMY BOOT CAMP

Rod Powers, retired Air Force sergeant

About the Expert: *Rod Powers retired from the Air Force in September 1998 with twenty-two years of service, eleven of those years as a first sergeant. He's been stationed around the world (both in Europe and Asia). Powers is the author of* ASVAB for Dummies, *and has been a featured speaker at various military ceremonies. His decorations include the Meritorious Service Medal with three oak-leaf clusters.*

Discipline and repetition are the hallmarks of boot camp. It is for this reason that new recruits can prepare themselves before they arrive and give themselves a leg up on their enlisted counterparts.

If you don't enjoy push-ups, then your arms will thank you if you take some time before arriving at boot camp to study about and practice the basics of military drills. There are countless books on this subject, and coming in with even a basic knowledge will make it less likely that you will become the target of a drill sergeant's wrath. It's also a good idea to get ahead of the game by memorizing Army officer and enlisted ranks, as well as the Army General Orders.

Get your body ready

Feeding the brain will certainly help in boot camp, but if you are not a physically active person, it's now time to get off the couch. Next to Marine Corps boot camp, Army basic training is the most physically intensive. You'll want to start preparing yourself a couple months before leaving for boot camp.

Concentrate on running, push-ups, and sit-ups, as these are the basis for the "pre-test" (thirteen push-ups, seventeen sit-ups, and a one-mile run in under eight and half minutes) and the final PT test.

Get used to being yelled at

Basic training is divided into three phases. During Phase I you will become acquainted with your drill sergeant. While the Army actually likes initiative and innovation, drill sergeants hate it. Soldiers arrive at their basic training unit and are immediately immersed into an environment where every move they make is scrutinized by the drill sergeant.

To avoid an embarrassing encounter with the drill sergeant during which he will go on at the top of his lungs about how he "works for a living," never address him as "sir." He is always to be addressed as "Yes, drill sergeant," delivered as loud as you can. Also never look him right in the eye as he will, without fail, ask if you are "eyeballing" him before ordering you to either run or perform push-ups until you vomit. Everyone has seen *Stripes*, so take a lesson from John Winger and don't piss off the drill sergeant.

Your average day

The typical basic training day runs from 0430 (4:30 A.M.) to 2100 (9 P.M.), so it would be a good idea to get yourself adjusted to the early day by keeping those hours for at least a few weeks before arriving.

Phase II is slightly better than Phase I. You'll learn how to throw grenades and fire your rifle. Of course you will be subjected to daily PT tests, as well as practice basic drills and ceremonies.

The most fun at basic training is had during Phase III. You'll have your final PT test and go camping. Without fail, during your camp in the field, your platoon will receive an "incoming" (a mock attack). It's a good idea (and it looks impressive) for the squad leaders and platoon leader to discuss this in advance and assign specific duties. Don't let the drill sergeants hear you planning this, though, as they are very good at making their own plans to thwart any of those that you may devise.

One thing to keep in mind during basic training is that thousands of men and women have gone through it before you and thousands will do so after you. It will be like going through hell, but it is nothing that can't be done. And when you are done, you'll be a part of the greatest military force on the planet.

Top Ten Tips for Surviving Boot Camp

1. Bring plenty of undergarments to get you through a week because having to do laundry is difficult, and finding an open washing machine is just as hard.
2. Get your hair cut before you leave home. The PX salons are about as great as having a three-year-old with a pair of scissors cut your hair.
3. Don't take any unneeded items with you, as drill sergeants aren't too keen on people who like to hide their contraband.
4. Get into shape before you leave home. You want your body to be prepared, not put into shock.
5. Vitamin C and menthol drops taste really good after not having anything sweet for a while. They are to trainees as cigarettes are to inmates.
6. Most units require you to buy new running shoes, so don't bother getting new ones before you go.
7. Only exercise when the drill sergeants tell you to. They don't want you getting hurt. It will drive you insane, but that's the way it is.

8. Practice the PT test. You can't graduate without passing it.
9. Don't bring any OTC medications. The Army will just take them from you. You can buy what you need from the Army.
10. Do what you are told.

48

HOW TO TALK TO YOUR KIDS ABOUT TOUGH TOPICS

Ethan Zohn, *Survivor* contestant, creator, Grassroots Soccer

About the Expert: *A former professional soccer player, Ethan Zohn used his winnings from* Survivor Africa *to start Grassroots Soccer, an organization that uses the sport to educate kids about AIDS and other subjects.*

What we are trying to accomplish with Grassroots Soccer is behavior change. What we do is attack difficult issues and tough things to talk to kids about through sports and fun activities. We use people who they identify with and respect.

In our educational and teaching sessions, the kids almost don't realize that they are learning. They do realize that we are talking about important stuff, but we do it in a manner and environment that are very comfortable for them.

We do poetry writing, and sometimes a kid who may not want to raise his hand and say, "What is a condom?" may express himself better in an essay or by writing a poem.

We do role-playing, also. Sometimes you're playing a part, and you're acting like a bully who is picking on a girl to pressure her into having sex. They're not really doing it, but they can approach the subject in a way they otherwise might not, because they're playing a role.

The key is to get the kids comfortable. In the beginning of our classes we have them sign a contract, saying that everything we say and do in the classroom stays in the classroom. We're not going to talk to anyone other than them about this stuff.

We're not going to go to their parents, and we're not going to go to their principal.

We have this honor code, this contract, and if you break a contract, just like in sports, you're going to get fired. Here, if we break this contract in this class, the same thing happens. When they are among their peers, they do feel comfortable, and if we need to separate the boys and girls, we will do that as well.

Sports helps

Using sports helps, because kids can relate to athletes. A lot of times you have a fifty- to sixty-year-old teacher standing up in front of a class saying, "Don't do this, and don't do that." But when you have young athletic sports players, kind of moderate stars with a little bit of celebrity status, it's a lot easier to get kids to listen.

I mean, these kids read about these players in magazines and watch them on TV and go to see them live. They are their role models. They are their heroes, and when you have these people delivering this message, the kids listen and understand. They can also identify with these players because they grew up in the same neighborhoods and the same environment.

I think that makes it much easier to bridge that gap because the kids don't feel like they are being preached to. There is a great quote from Nelson Mandela that exemplifies what we are trying to do: "Sport has the power to change the world, the power to unite people in a way that little else can. Sport can create hope where there was once despair. It is an instrument for peace even more powerful than governments. It breaks down racial barriers. It laughs in the face of all kinds of discrimination. The heroes sport creates are examples of this power. They are valiant, not only on the playing field, but also in the community, spreading hope and inspiration to the world." That is pretty much what we try to do.

Don't talk down

I have always felt like you should talk to kids as though they were adults. Obviously you will want to simplify the facts and get the general information out there. But if you talk down to them, if you baby them, you'll turn them off.

If you just give them the facts, talk to them like they're your friends, talk to them like you're thinking, This is not embarrassing for me to talk about, and it should not be embarrassing for you to talk about, I find that there is an equal respect there. They feel mature; they feel important when you talk to them about these important subjects in a way that is not dumbing it down for them.

Sex is a tough subject to talk to kids about. Anytime you bring up the subject of sex with children, there is always that thin line, as if, if you talk about it, maybe you're promoting it and sending people out to go and do it. But basically I think they need to be given all the information possible.

We give these kids all the information, and we let them make the decision to lead a healthy lifestyle. We arm them with the information for them to make the right choices. And that is the point we're trying to get at. Sometimes they don't have the right information and they are making the wrong choices.

Know what your kids know

We have both pre and post questionnaires that Stanford University helped us to create for kids in the program. It is all about the evaluation process. The funny thing is that we find out the kids already know a lot. You need to know what your kids know.

Kids memorize facts, but they don't know how to apply those facts. It's like giving someone a meal, along with a knife, fork, and spoon, but not showing them how to use the utensils. They know what it is used for, just not how to use it. These kids know how AIDS is spread—though sex, and blood, and sharp objects—but they don't know how that comes up in real life. We provide practicality to those facts.

Don't wait to talk to your kids about these issues, or rely on schools to do it. Schools are waiting until seventh, eighth, even ninth grade to teach these things, and by then it may be too late.

Have no agenda

Don't try to influence the kids to go one way or the other. I can't go in there and say, "You need to abstain from sex," or "You can't drink."

A kid will find himself in a situation in which he'll have to decide if he's going to have a drink, or if he's going to have sex. If all he has is you saying "no, no, no," then he'll probably go ahead and do it. But if has just the straight info, then the odds that he'll make the right choice are greater.

49

HOW TO HANDLE BEING ARRESTED

Jack Bradley, attorney

About the Expert: *Jack Bradley is a criminal defense attorney with a practice in Lorain, Ohio. He has represented countless clients accused of serious crimes, including murder.*

The most important thing to do when you are arrested is to not talk to the police. In my practice I find that it is usually not a good thing for people talk to the police. A lot of times the police do not understand what the person is trying to say, or they misinterpret what the person is trying to say. Later on, that misinterpretation works against the person who has been arrested.

The smartest lawyers in America are on the United States Supreme Court, and basically, they told people in the 1960s that if you are questioned by the police after you've been arrested, keep your big mouth shut. They didn't say it that way; they said that people who are arrested have to be informed by the police that they have the right to remain silent and anything that they do say can and will be used against them.

Really, what the judges on the Supreme Court are saying to the people is "Don't talk to the police." The reason behind that is that the law doesn't say, "Anything you say can and will be used to help you." It says, "Anything you say will be used against you." Even though everybody knows about his or her Miranda Rights, it seems as though when people get arrested, they tend to forget about that right to remain silent.

Instead, the person getting arrested wants to start talking to the police right away. Your first Miranda Right is to keep your big mouth shut. People seem to remember that more than, "You have the right to remain silent."

Really, be quiet

The police tell people, "Well, you know, if you don't have anything to hide, then you should probably be talking to us." That is exactly the wrong advice. If you don't have anything to hide, that is more of a reason to keep quiet.

An example of that was in the case of the runaway bride. The police initially thought she was abducted or kidnapped, or that something else happened to her that was criminal in nature. So right away the police wanted to give a polygraph test to the fiancé. Well, his father is a judge and he said, Whoa, wait a minute, we had better get you an attorney, and you are not going to talk to the police until we get some advice from an attorney.

Of course the attorney said, Well, you are not going to take a police polygraph test. We're going to have certain rules that we'll set up and we'll have that polygraph test set up not at a police station, but at a neutral location, and we are going to pick the expert who is going to give the polygraph test. Naturally, the police didn't like that, and right away they started accusing the fiancé of having something to hide.

As it turns out, he was doing the right thing by not talking, because his future bride did run away, and he didn't do anything wrong.

Once you're inside

Try to get hold of a family member as soon as possible and have that family member get hold of an attorney so that the attorney can get down to the police station and give you some advice on what you should do. Normally, the attorney would give you advice on how to post a bond, what you are going to be looking at when you get to court, and how quickly you can get to court. It is very important to get hold of that family member as quickly as you can.

Most police departments have a bond schedule. Depending on the offense that you are charged with, they may allow you to just sign your name. Your signature would be enough to guarantee that you are going to show up for your court appearance. Normally for something like petty theft, or even DUI, that is enough.

For a more serious offense such as a felony, a bond may not even be set. In that case you appear before the judge on the next available court date. You will sit in jail until the judge sets a bond. Then you will post that amount of money in cash.

If the bond was $2,500, you would have to deposit $2,500 with the clerk of the court, or sometimes the court will accept a bondsman, who is paid a premium to guarantee that amount of money. He would be paid 10 percent of the bond amount as his fee for guaranteeing that money if you did not appear in court.

Does it matter if you did it?

No, not really. Basically, your attorney will want to hear what you have to say. The best advice is to be truthful with the attorney, whether you did or did not do something. You should be truthful with the attorney so that he knows the facts of the case. Your attorney will then do what he thinks is necessary to properly defend you.

Treat the police right

The only thing you can do while you are being arrested is try to be as polite and cooperative as possible and not get to the point where you call the officer names or make demands on the officer. Sometimes it is an emotionally charged situation, and the officer's adrenaline is rushing, and if you do anything that could set him off he may react in an inappropriate way. Call the officer sir or ma'am.

It is really hard to prove that an officer has overstepped his bounds. All you can really do is hope that the officer doesn't go over the boundary lines and is in complete control. Remember, he has the gun, he has you in handcuffs, he has the stun-gun and the pepper spray, he has all the tools that are necessary to subdue you, and it is very, very foolish to think that you can begin making demands or trying to put up resistance, and that it will work to your benefit.

Search me

They can't search your home unless they have a warrant or your permission. But if they decide that they want to do it regardless, allow them to perform the search. Later you can challenge them in court, nothing that they did not have a search warrant. That is why it is so important that you tell the police right away that you don't want to talk, so that at no point can they say that you did give your permission for a search.

Your car is different. There is less need for a search warrant to search a car. So if you are arrested, you can count on getting your car searched, and that it will be a legal search.

Comport yourself well

When you are in court, dress like you are going to an important event, especially if you are going to appear before the judge. (There are plenty of times that you may go to court and sit in the hallway while your attorney makes the appearance for you.)

You should always check with your attorney as to what he thinks is appropriate. Personally, I don't like my clients to wear suits because that is generally not something that they wear every day and they find the suits uncomfortable. So I tell them to wear something that they might wear to church, to a funeral, or to an event that would be more dressy. I tell them to wear a nice pair of pants, dress shoes, and a nice shirt. A tie or sports coat is really optional.

They should always be polite and cooperative. When addressing the judge, it should always be "Yes your honor; no your honor." But most of the talking should be done by the attorney. It is also a good idea to have a lot of family members there. People have a tendency to have more faith or trust in someone who has their family there showing support for them.

TV is not reality

I know a lot of prosecutors and a lot of police officers who are upset with shows like *CSI*, because they believe that people now think that a crime can be solved in one hour and that police should use DNA and fingerprints in every case.

Remember, it is the government's job to prove that you did something wrong. You do not have to prove your innocence. If the police don't have enough evidence, it is likely that the case will be dismissed before it ever goes to trial. So remember that the government is the one pointing the finger at you, and they have to prove the case. You don't have to prove a negative.

50

HOW TO SURVIVE TIME IN PRISON

Edward Bales, chief psychologist,
Federal Prison Consultants

About the Expert: *Edward Bales is chief psychologist for Federal Prison Consultants. FPC was established approximately ten years ago as federal and state advocates and sentencing specialists. They are leaders in the field of federal and state prison-reduction strategies.*

The first thing you need to do is to prepare yourself mentally and emotionally for the fact that you are going to have to do your time. Once you've done that, things will be a little bit easier; it gives you a little sense of peace.

People who are incarcerated tell people when they come in to do the time and not let the time do you. That means: Come in, surrender yourself to the fact that you are there and that you are going to have to bite the bullet and do the course of action and get in and get out as fast as possible and get back to a productive life.

Acceptance is hard

It seems like half the people accept the situation and do what they have to do and the other half fight it. Some people go in and usually end up fighting their sentence from the beginning to the time that they leave. They cause infractions and get into trouble and don't do what they should be doing, which is concentrating on taking as much educational programming as they can. Take advantage of the system. Make sure you get yourself mentally and physically taken care of. Use the medical facilities that are available to you in prison. There are a lot of different programs available in prison, like work programs that give you training toward a trade. We recommend that you jump at the chance to take advantage of any program that is offered to you in prison.

How bad is it?

It depends on the level of the prison that you are going into. Most of our clients are either first-time offenders or going into minimal-security camps or minimum-security facilities where the violence factor is low. These are people who committed small drug crimes, have never used a gun, and don't know what a gun is like: white-collar criminals who just don't have a violent nature to them at all.

Then there is the medium- or high-security facility, that is, what you see on TV and hear about in prison stories. Basically what you have to do when you are going into that type of facility is be careful not to drop the soap in the shower.

To stay out of situations like that, you have to present yourself as someone who you are not. You may have to present yourself as someone who can defend himself. You'll have to keep quiet. You certainly don't want to show off or brag. You want to keep the lowest profile possible. That is the only thing you can do.

Sometimes you may find yourself in a situation where you can't control what happens. Sometimes you end up in what they call protective custody. And that protects you from that type of environment. However, you're stuck in a cell twenty-four hours a day, and you have supervised visits or exercise for maybe an hour out of the day.

Get your life in order

Most people don't have the time to get their personal lives in order before going to jail. What we suggest is that if they have some type of substance-abuse problem, they seek appropriate help on the outside to help them to integrate and adjust in prison. This may help them to qualify for programs that they may not have otherwise qualified for.

If they have an alcohol or drug problem, we recommend that they complete a 12-step program like AA. If they have gambling problems, they should start going to Gamblers Anonymous. If they have a sexual problem, they should seek help from private therapy and document it.

Not always what you expect

What prison is like depends on the level of security that you are placed in. If you are placed in a camp-style facility, your schedule is really only regimented during your working hours. Your working hours are anywhere from two to six hours a day, based on what you do.

You will probably never see a bar in a camp, just a regular window. It will look like a college campus. Some of the facilities have soda in the dining areas; there are vending machines; there are microwave ovens; you are able to move about inside and outside of the compound. You can jog; there are walking grounds; you can play sports like volleyball, bocce, and horseshoes. There are even gardens where you can grow vegetables. There are no walls. You could actually walk away if you chose to, but eventually you'd get caught.

In the higher-level prisons, on the other hand, you have a very regimented schedule. You can only move on the hour to different parts of the facility. You have to wait to be told to move.

You can even get into situations in the highest-level compounds where the inmate is, in fact, retained in their cell for the majority of the time. They are allowed out to a compound for recreation, but this is very restricted. If you get into the super-high-security prisons, like the one that John Gotti was in, you are confined to your cell twenty-four hours a day. Your existence is very, very limited. You do get half an hour a day to go out-side or take a shower, but even then the shower is a machine that bathes you. You are not allowed in the regular showers.

A long time

If you have a long sentence, you have to prepare yourself for the fact that you may never get out. One thing that some peo-ple do is make sure that they exhaust every possible appeals route.

Be careful

Mind your own business, don't talk about your crime, and don't ask anyone else about theirs.

Two of the biggest areas of conflict are the telephone and the television. Inmates fight over telephone use and they fight over what channel they are going to watch in the TV rooms. Stay away from the telephones, stay away from the TV rooms. And if you are in those rooms, be very respectful.

Believe it or not, in a higher-level prison, there is actually something to the idea that you should kick somebody's ass on the first day. But if you are in a low- or minimal-security facil-ity, you don't want to get into a fight. If you do, you will be placed in a higher-level facility. If you are in a higher-level prison, I wouldn't want to go so far as to say to get into a fight on the first day, but I would say to you that I would think you would want to show to the other inmates that you are able to defend yourself.

You don't have to start a fight, but you should be prepared to say that you won't take any crap and that you're there to do your time. I wouldn't recommend actually getting into a fight, unless you are defending yourself, and in that situation, you have to do what you have to do.

Defend yourself

You have to defend yourself in prison, and usually that means you have to do it with your fists. Some people in prison make what they call shanks. These are made out of all different kinds of materials, like toothbrushes and razor blades, and they can be deadly weapons.

Steer clear of prison gangs. They exist, and they are certainly part of higher-level security prisons, but they are not really a part of the lower-level prisons. They do present themselves to the inmate population and they do put you under their wing and protect you, but it works both ways. Those types of groups get into fights with other groups. So you may not be in a one-on-one situation, but you could be faced with multitudes of people fighting. The best thing is to avoid all that, do your time, keep to yourself, and stay as low-key as possible.

That applies not only to the inmate population, but to the guards as well. The more the staff sees you, the more they associate you as being a problem. If they don't know who you are, they like that. They don't want to know who you are.

Acknowledgments

This book would not have been possible without the unwavering support of our wives, Dawn Tomaszewski and Celine Provini. More than any of the people involved in this process, they had to suffer through the endless phone calls, nights spent in front of a computer, and our general lack of availability. In addition to our spouses, many family members and friends also had to deal with canceled plans, holidays missed, and life events not celebrated because we were waiting by the phone in case Dustin "Screech" Diamond called (sadly, he never did).

We also received a lot of support from our coworkers at Lynn Ladder & Scaffolding, specifically Eileen Fabish, Leo Otero, Lester Ojeda, Luis Rivera, Jose Gonzalez, and Jazmin Otero in New Haven, Connecticut, and Steve Young, Duane Boucher, Ed Downey, Mark Krook, Joe Riccio, Mark Botta, Tom Berta, Kris Gagnon, Deborah Hines, and Frank Koughan at our other locations. Their efforts have helped us realize our goal of being the most successful authors in the ladder and scaffolding industry.

A number of other people, including our brothers, Todd Kline and Matt Tomaszewski, helped or supported this project, including Kevin Young, Kaitlin McCallum, Lin Noble, Leigh Bogle, Sarah Caron, Sonja Zinke, and Mr. T, whose compassion for fools has always been an inspiration to us. We'd also like to thank Dan's son (Jason's godson) Joshua, who was too young to be helpful, but will soon be old enough for us to not want him to read certain chapters.

Dan would like to thank Jeff Colchamiro for his constant support throughout his writing career. He would also like to thank Erik Cavagnuolo, J. R. Taylor, Daniela Stinger, Michael Malone, Karen Pantelides, Mike Denapoli, Jerry Beach, David Becker, and the rest of the Rouze team for putting him in a position to be considered a men's lifestyle expert.

Jason would like to thank Mike and Lynette Majesky, Tim Alcorn, Terrilyn Tomaszewski, and Mark Tomaszewski for their help and support of this project. He would also like to thank Andrew and Shannon Dubinsky, Matt Stasko, Adam Thermann, Joe DeMaria, Chris Longo, Jeff Garner, and the rest of the G-4 guys for sharing many of the experiences that helped inspire this book.

Our agents at Venture Literary, Frank Scatoni and Greg Dinkin, also deserve a lot of credit, since we never would have even written the proposal for this book if they had not pushed for it. And, of course, we thank our editor, Jake Klisivitch, and the rest of the team at Plume, whose faith in this project kept us going.